Thrival Skills 101

Path to Joy...
Moving from Survival to Thrival

Charlotte F. LeHecka, PhD

BALBOA.PRESS
A DIVISION OF HAY HOUSE

Balboa Press books may be ordered through booksellers or by contacting:

Balboa Press
A Division of Hay House
1663 Liberty Drive
Bloomington, IN 47403
www.balboapress.com
844-682-1282

Because of the dynamic nature of the Internet, any web addresses or links contained in this book may have changed since publication and may no longer be valid. The views expressed in this work are solely those of the author and do not necessarily reflect the views of the publisher, and the publisher hereby disclaims any responsibility for them.

The author of this book does not dispense medical advice or prescribe the use of any technique as a form of treatment for physical, emotional, or medical problems without the advice of a physician, either directly or indirectly. The intent of the author is only to offer information of a general nature to help you in your quest for emotional and spiritual well-being. In the event you use any of the information in this book for yourself, which is your constitutional right, the author and the publisher assume no responsibility for your actions.

Any people depicted in stock imagery provided by Getty Images are models, and such images are being used for illustrative purposes only. Certain stock imagery © Getty Images.

Print information available on the last page.

ISBN: 978-1-9822-7600-3 (sc)
ISBN: 978-1-9822-7601-0 (e)

Balboa Press rev. date: 11/18/2021

CONTENTS

I dedicate this book to my three children—Nana,
Samantha and Zack—my teachers.

ACKNOWLEDGEMENTS

I'd like to begin by acknowledging the Spirit within us all. It is that Spirit which fuels our passions, fills our hearts with dreams and visions and gives us the strength to pursue our deepest desires. In my case, I owe a deep debt of gratitude to the many explorers of the human spirit who have impacted my life in profound ways. They are: Colin Tipping, author of *Radical Forgiveness*, who by teaching me that there is never anything or anyone to forgive, radically changed the trajectory of my life. Marshall Rosenberg, whose book *Nonviolent Communication* gave me a way to share what is alive in me while also honoring the needs of the other. I want to thank Edwene Gaines for helping me understand how much God wants us all to succeed and Myrtle Fillmore for teaching me how to live and how to die. I have been so grateful to Ellen Debenport for her take on Unity's Five Principles. So many of her life experiences paralleled my own that her story-telling really brought the principles to life for me. And last but not least, Lee Coit, whose little books—*Listening, Accepting, Being* and *Awakening*—I go back to over and over again when I'm feeling stuck and need a reminder of what it's all about.

I also have a number of dear friends and family members whom I want to thank. I received invaluable feedback about ways to improve this book from my friend and amazing author Lynn Harris and my daughter Samantha Brown, who has the clarity and insight to see things from a different perspective. My friend Emily Millett has been my cheerleader as well as a giver of feedback along with a dear friend of hers, Rev. Cate Howell whose feedback I also took to heart. To my proof-readers—my sister, Jennie Walker, and my good friend, Jane Burgess—who did the final edit, I say: "Thank you." I feel very fortunate to have had Laura Morris, a graphic designer friend of mine, give me valuable input on the book cover. And last but not least, I want to thank the staff at Balboa Press—Melanie Foursha, Michael March, Lucas Biery, Adolfo Loremas, Ginna Akita Pastorfide, and Aaron Hurwitz—with whom I worked for their encouragement, patience, and support.

I also want to acknowledge my spiritual community, Unity in Greensboro, who has given me the space to write. They have picked up the slack during my sabbatical with grace and dedication. I have had the good fortune during the pandemic to be a part of two book study groups and a prayer group who have been my support group. Thank you Jeannine, Suki, Suzanne, Lina, Barbara, Gayla, Laurie, Seema, Lynn, Ellie, Jane, and Rick. And thank you Zoom!

INTRODUCTION

LIFE IS ABOUT THRIVING

Life is not just about surviving, it's about thriving. This book will give you the skills—if you commit to practice—to change your consciousness. As a metaphysician, I understand that there are different levels of consciousness. There is the physical level and there is the spiritual level. God's creations are always spiritual. Humankind's creations are both material and spiritual. As we learn to upgrade our consciousness so that we are interacting with the world more from our spiritual level of consciousness than our physical level of consciousness, we will have a different and more rewarding experience of our here and now. As the saying goes: *Change your consciousness, change your life.*

There are a number of skills that you will be learning in the pages of this book, but the first and most important is learning to quiet the mind. "Why" you might ask is this so important? It's important because until you learn to quiet the "monkey chatter" that goes on 24/7, you don't have the control you need to change your thinking. AND it is only when you change your thinking that you change your life.

Over the duration of this book, we will look at five specific areas of growth that all of us must master if we are to live lives of "joy". They are:

- Connecting to our Essence
- Getting to know Ourselves—an On-Purpose Life
- Relationships with Self and Others
- Evolving a Prosperity Consciousness
- Vibrating with Health

Each of the chapters covers one of these areas of growth with the exception of the topic of Relationships with Self and Others. It is covered in two chapters: Empowering Relationships and Interpersonal Relationships and Communication. Each chapter is divided into three sections. The first section entitled **Prose** tells a story. The second section is called **Principle.** It addresses the underlying principles being highlighted in the **Prose** section. And the third section is about **Practice.** This third section supports one of my guiding beliefs: *It is not enough to know the Truth, we must put that Truth into action in our lives.*

The concepts in this book are not new. All great spiritual leaders from all faith traditions have espoused these principles and practices in one form or another. Yet, each of us is different and we each learn differently. I learn through stories. This book is for those of you, who like me, deepen their understanding of how to move from survival to thrival through stories.

After reading this book and practicing the principles described, your life will be changed forever. You will never be able to go back to simply existing in the conditioned life you were living.

You will be empowered by your connection with Source Energy and an understanding of Universal Principles/Laws. You will tap the unlimited depths of your spiritual beingness and learn how to release old thought patterns and illuminate the path to a life of infinite possibilities.

These practices help you uncover and face your fears. This is a good thing! As you heal the layers of fear, you ascend—transforming your mind, body and spirit.

As you work your way through these materials, you may find that some of the topics seem to be repeating themselves. Let that be okay for repetition from a slightly different perspective helps us deepen our understanding.

In many cases, the practices are easy to apply. In others, they may present more of a challenge. Yet, they do give you a roadmap to help you discover where your next step needs to be. From time to time, the lessons will refer you to other authors who have explicated a concept and developed additional practices to help you on your journey.

So, now it's time to say "good-bye" to a life of lack, limitation, and fear and say "hello" to a life of unconditional love and infinite possibilities. Say with me, I,_____, now set the intention to heal the fear within me and live the life I was destined to live. I am open to receive. I allow Infinite Source to work through me as me. And, as I have spoken, so it is!

GLOSSARY OF TERMS

Consciousness—There are three different ways to understand consciousness. When we refer to Universal Consciousness, we understand it to mean the creation of form from formlessness. When we talk about global consciousness, we are referring to the collective thoughts and feelings of all sentient beings. When we refer to consciousness at the level of the individual, we are referring to the many different levels of consciousness from lower levels of human consciousness where we feel that life is against us to higher levels of consciousness which we refer to as our Higher or Christ Consciousness. At this level of consciousness, we are in constant contact with the Divinity within and do not experience separation.

God—When I reference God in this book, I am understanding God as Source Energy—a benevolent, creative life force underlying all creation. On occasion, I may also refer to God as Universal Energy, Infinite Oneness, Infinite Love, Universal Spirit, ALL THAT IS, and the Ground of All.

Universal Principles—Our universe is an orderly universe run on certain unalterable principles. They operate whether we are aware of them or not. Gravity, for example, is a physical law or principle. Just so, there are spiritual laws or principles that operate whether we are consciously aware of them or not. If we take all the different spiritual laws and principles man has identified, they all really boil down to an understanding that before there is form, there is consciousness. It is our thoughts and feelings that create our reality. So the universal principle is a process that begins with thought and ends with an outcome that aligns with that thought.

Jesus—a human being just like the rest of us. Jesus is our Wayshower. He demonstrates through his life how to stay connected with Source Energy, God, and he also teaches us how to do the same.

Christ Consciousness—Christ Consciousness as a concept is interchangeable with Higher Self or Christ Spirit.

Law of Mind Action—This is also often called the Law of Attraction. This law states that we attract into our lives whatever we predominantly put our focus and our attention upon.

The Silence—is that inner place of stillness where you feel and know your oneness with God. Often, this text will use the expression "going into the Silence". This refers to our decision to meditate, to shut out the outer world and enter the inner world where we connect with our Divinity.

ONE

CONNECTING TO OUR ESSENCE

Prose

*The greatest thing is, at any given moment,
to be willing to give up who we are in
order to become all that we can be.*

—Max De Pree

Many authors have suggested that our spiritual journeys are usually kickstarted by some event that creates a crisis in our lives causing us to question the values and beliefs we have held up until that point. My seminal experience began when I became a high school exchange student in Germany at the age of seventeen.

In our youth program at church we were looking at different opportunities open for young people and I chose to make a report on the International Christian Youth Exchange Program (ICYE). From the moment I read about it, I felt this bubbling up in me, this feeling of aliveness and anticipation and I just knew this was something I needed to do.

According to my parents, being an exchange student was something I just kept coming back to over and over again for an entire year. I don't remember that exactly, but it must have been true because they decided that this desire was simply not going to go away and made a commitment to support me in this adventure. And it was a huge commitment on their part as it wasn't just about my going to live in Germany for a year, it also meant my family would be adopting an exchange student into our family for a year.

Once they gave me the go-ahead, my job was to get the support of our congregation too which was one of the many steps the program required. And that meant financially. I remember getting up in front of the congregation, sharing information about ICYE and asking for support in making this dream a reality. Little did I know at the time that this experience would be such a life changer for me. I just knew it was something I needed to do.

Growing up in a small town in Mississippi, I loved participating in the life of our church. I enjoyed being with my friends in Sunday School, attending Sunday morning and evening services, singing in the choir and attending all the social functions. I also believed I was grounded in scripture, and although I did have some problems with some of the Bible's stories, all in all I was a pretty happy camper. Being a Methodist, I even grew up imagining myself someday becoming a missionary. And then Germany happened.

To be specific, I was accepted into the church sponsored International Christian Youth Exchange Program (ICYE). Through this program, I lived with this amazing family, the Dörings for a year, and attended Friedrich-List-Schule Wirtshaftsgymnasium (Economics-oriented High School). In the German high school, religion was one of our required classes. Just imagine what it must have been like for a young girl from Mississippi who had been totally insulated in her community coming into an environment where students openly defied or denied Christianity. There were both atheists and agnostics in my class and they were not at all shy about asking me all kinds of questions about my beliefs. I found myself trying to defend a way of believing that I was not so well versed in as I thought. My belief system crumbled.

I didn't know where to turn and felt lost. In hindsight, I have words to describe this experience of going into the void, but at the time I only knew that what I had believed wasn't working for me anymore and I had no idea how to fill this void. Now I understand that what I perceived as loss in my life was simply another layer of awakening. But at the time, the dismantling of my world created disorientation, and I longed for the old, familiar ways that seemed to work.

For a period of about ten years, using scholarships and fellowships, I went back and forth between the United States and Germany trying to sort it all out. Finally, I realized I couldn't go back to the teachings of the church I had grown up in, but I wasn't sure where to turn. So, I began reading and reading and reading—paying attention to those things that made sense to me. Through that process I developed my own spiritual path, but I didn't know anyone who shared similar beliefs as mine.

Then one day I was taking a class in Silva Mind Control and a student in the class said to me: "If you think this is great, then you should visit Unity." I was like: "Lady, you don't understand, my feet have not graced a church in eleven years. I don't think so." However, one of the things I have come to appreciate is that the Universe ALWAYS has our back. And, as fate would have it, about three months later I found myself at the Pyramid in Houston and as I listened, I KNEW I had found a new spiritual home. What a surprise it was to discover so many other like-minded people. In fact, even today Unity's core principles still inform my spiritual journey.

You might ask, how can I be so certain that my soul had finally found a home? To that I answer: "You know when you know". There are no questions. No need to analyze or explain. You just know. I am certain that each of you reading this book has had a similar experience at one time or another in your life. It's certainly happened to me on numerous other occasions.

Did you know that these experiences are our soul's way of giving us a nudge? Of opening us up to new possibilities. I see it as a knock on the door saying: "It's time to expand your consciousness, time to learn more about who you really are and how you—in particular—are being called to add to the love quotient in our world." Listening to these knowings is our way of developing a custom-designed learning curriculum to assure our soul's maximum growth and development. In fact, my whole German experience was most assuredly a "soul" call.

Principle

In this next section, we explore five core spiritual teachings. These are the foundational stones for the journey we are embarking on together. All of the other principles and practices grow out of them. In describing these five principles, I draw heavily upon the work of Ellen Debenport. Having used her book, *The Five Principles,* to teach our Foundation's class at Unity many, many times over the past fifteen years, it's sometimes challenging for me to determine where her words leave off and mine begin.

As we saw in the above two stories, the soul gets our attention in two ways: 1) by planting seeds of desire in our hearts, or 2) by allowing what appear to us as crises to happen when it's time for us to open ourselves up to an even greater understanding of what "unconditional love" looks like as it is expressed through each of us.

My first story of becoming an exchange student represents a response to a heart-felt desire. In my second story, I share the challenges I experienced as my old way of relating to God ended, what my time in the void was like and then the joy of a new beginning. One could describe these events as a "crisis" but I now prefer to understand the event as my soul calling me forth to grow and expand.

Hopefully, each of these two stories sparked an insight of a time in your past when you saw a situation as a crisis which now, with hindsight, you understand was for your benefit, or a time you just knew something was your next RIGHT step. I would like to make the claim that we know when we know because of our God connection.

Depending upon where you are in your journey, your sense of your God connection, i.e. your understanding that God and you are one, may be more or less self-evident to you. And that's okay, because each of us is at a different place in our journey and wherever we are is perfect for us.

How do I know that? Because it's where we are. We are not somewhere else. I am experiencing this moment and this moment is the moment I'm supposed to be experiencing. If I were meant to experience something else, I would be experiencing something else. In fact, most of the suffering we experience in life is because we want something to be other than the way it is. As we go through this journey together, a big part of what we will be learning is to—as Byron Katie says so eloquently—Love What Is! I welcome you on our journey.

Core Teaching One: God is good and everywhere present.

Let me ask you a question: Is it really necessary to define God in order to know God? I know it's been important to me to think about God and I have seen my understanding of God shift from an image of a God who was sometimes vengeful, a God that I would want to hide my true thoughts and feelings from, to an understanding of God that I refer to as Source Energy nowadays.

It's been pretty self-evident from the many different religious traditions that we humans have always sensed some invisible foundation to the universe. Science has shown us that there is an implicate order and an explicate order to the universe. This implicate order is what I call Source Energy or ALL THAT IS. When I think of God as Source Energy I understand it as the energy, the creative life force underlying all creation. This eternal life force cannot be an entity or supreme being having opinions or judgments. And since we all have the freedom to create our own stories about the nature of God and the Universe, I choose to see this energy source as an ever-evolving, benevolent, restorative energy out of which all created things and beings are made.

So, why do I say Source Energy is "ever-evolving, benevolent, and restorative." Because when I look out on our planet at the trees, the plants, the birds, the animals, when I take in a beautiful sunrise or sunset or look out at the Universe with its billions of stars and planets, when I think of the miracle of our own bodies even, I see a vastness and an order to the Universe that is both unfathomable, exhilarating and ever-evolving.

When doctors put a broken bone back together or give some medication or supplements to support our healing, the doctor does not do the healing. It's the Universal Energy which is around us and in us as us that does the healing.

And lastly, how do I know that the Universe is benevolent? Because we can know God in the stillness. In my own experience in meditation, I have lost all sense of self and have known myself to be one with the Infinite Oneness, the Infinite Love that is God. After such an experience, there is again no doubt, you know what you know. You know what it feels like to be in the energy of unconditional love.

Understanding God as Love freed me from that childhood image of God as a supreme being with opinions and judgments. The key to my understanding of God today is that God is love and only love—that the entire universe is "for" me. And when I experience anything contradictory to that, I must look inside to determine how I have chosen to believe that I am separate from the love, the goodness, the allness that is God.

On our journey, we will discover that there are spiritual laws just as there are physical laws. And when we break those spiritual laws there are consequences. We will also learn something else: unconditional love trumps even spiritual laws.

You might ask, how can you say God is good and everywhere present when we look around us and see so much stuff going on that does not appear to be good? To answer this question we need to continue our exploration of the other core teachings.

Core Teaching Two: Human Beings inherent nature is also good.

The principle of Oneness—that we are in God and God is in us, that we are one with each other and the entire universe, is for many of us a far reach. What does it mean when we say that everything, absolutely everything and everyone is divine? The most common question I get is: If God is good and God is all there is, how can evil exist in the world?

Traditional Christianity teaches that humans are born sinful. But to believe that we must refute Core Teaching One which says that God is all good and everywhere present. If this is so as we explored in our discussion of Core Teaching One, then God cannot be some places and not others. Everywhere is everywhere! That means that God is in you and you are in God. I like to actually refer to us as Godlings!!!

Through loving consciousness, all things were created, including this manifest world. Can you imagine God creating something that is not inherently good? I can't. Not when, as mentioned above, I look about me and see the results of Its expressing in every growing plant, tree, and living creature.

So if—as the scripture says: "We are perfect even as our Father in heaven is perfect" (Mathew 5:48), how can we make sense of the fact that our world does not appear to be perfect? It's a question that theologians and ordinary people alike have wrestled with since time in memoriam. In her book, *The Five Principles,* Ellen Debenport gives us a number of possible ways we could think about that question. Below are a few examples of what others have proposed:

- Humans were created with free will, and we make mistakes. The word sin originally meant missing the mark and some people miss it by miles!

- Good and evil are simply labels that humans give to events based on our opinions at the time. What first appears as a tragedy may turn out to be a blessing.
- The human species is immature. The Aramaic word that has been translated as evil in the Bible actually means "immature" or "unripe".
- We can't see the big picture. Events have meaning we do not understand, although later we might see the gifts that were brought to us through the most difficult times in our lives.
- We are creating our world through consciousness (Core Teaching Three), which most people do not realize, much less know how to handle. Our every thought, feeling and word sets up a response from the universe, but we have only a glimmer of understanding about how to create our experience deliberately.
- What we call evil is an expression of mass consciousness. We all contribute to it through our angry and violent thoughts, the energetic vibrations we pour out into the One Mind.
- We are balancing the events of a past life, sometimes called karma. This is not so much punishment or reward as reconciling accounts and offering us an opportunity to experience life from all sides. [1]

These theories reflect the imperfection of us humans, but these theories do not provide evidence for another power. When we try to put our actions off on a force outside of ourselves we are simply choosing not to take responsibility for our actions. Often we hear people say: "Well, I am only human." While it may support us in the moment to believe this way, if we accept the truth of Core Teaching One that God is everywhere present, then, in our hearts, we know that this is simply not true.

Yes, we are having a human experience and, yes because of the truths millions of humans before us have slowly brought into the world, our understanding of the evolutionary process and our place in it continues to expand. Each generation throughout history has been serving to evolve human reality in a purposeful way, bringing us ever closer to the spiritual awareness that is our true birthright. Step by step we are becoming aware that we ARE spiritual beings slowly evolving into the spiritual reality

God implanted in us from the very beginning. So, just keep saying to yourself: "I am a spiritual being having a human experience. I am a spiritual being having a human experience. I am a spiritual being having a human experience." And know that each time we take these words deep into our consciousness, it becomes more and more a reality for us.

Another story from Debenport's book has been helpful in wrapping my mind around this idea that we are one with God, the Ground of All. Imagine that God is the ocean and we are the droplets; therefore, our essence and the essence of Source are the same. [2] Our only job in life is to be aware of and responsive to that presence both within and around us. I can trust, that as I attune myself to the essence within, I will be guided and directed in ways that free my spirit to live life fully. Recently, I have actually learned that no matter what I do, the Universe is so benevolent; it even takes those experiences I label "mistakes" and turns them around.

Since God is both transcendent (all there is, everywhere) and immanent (personal, within), our personal relationship with the Divine dwells within us as our superconscious. It is through the Spirit within that we know our oneness with God. We are the Divine expressing in human form. It is our job as human beings to revive this spiritual truth in the world and to live from the Center of our being, the part of us that knows itself to be God expressing, our divine core.

Every human being knows this Self already, at least to some extent. It is the inner witness that watches our life unfold and is conscious of our existence. It is the intuitive nudge like the situation I described in my story above which prompts us to go a new and different way. Yes, we are talking about that still, small voice inside of us that is willing to give us guidance and direction if we but ask for it. In Core Teaching Four we will explore how we go about getting and staying in touch with our Higher Self.

Let's be clear. We do not have a soul; we are a soul that has a body and an ego. Because our soul is an eternal, individualized creation, it has a mandate to grow, learn and evolve into an ever-closer union with God. Imagine how much faster we would evolve if we put the soul in charge of our lives instead of our ego. Many people believe we need to rid ourselves of our ego, but that is simply not true. What we do need to do is to bring the ego in service to the soul. As we progress in our studies together, we will learn a number of practices we can use which are designed to nurture the soul and bring forth Spirit in each of us.

But let's imagine for a moment a time before our physical incarnation when we were wandering the heavens as a discarnate soul. We were enjoying ourselves immensely when a call came out for volunteers to incarnate in bodily, human form. We make the decision to volunteer. We next meet with the Incarnation Committee to discuss with its members the part we want to play and the work we want to accomplish. We have many decisions to make; we have to decide what particular set of gifts, talents and abilities we wish to bring with us to contribute to life on earth and we also have to determine what situations and conflicts might be most beneficial in helping us learn, grow and develop ourselves in some area.

Maybe, we decide we want to learn about forgiveness in this incarnation or perhaps we want to learn about the use of power or practice unconditional love. Once the decisions are made and all the other players such as our parents and siblings have agreed to do their part in bringing us the lessons and resources we need, it's time to depart. To bring this home, let me share a little story from *The Little Soul and the Sun* by Neale Donald Walsh. In his story a little soul is planning a human lifetime to work on forgiveness. Another soul offers to accompany him to Earth. "I will help you," she says. "I can come into your next lifetime and do something for you to forgive!" [3] So, perhaps now we can better understand why the most difficult people in our lives, the ones that push our buttons, are sometimes considered our greatest teachers. Maybe Hitler and Osama Bin Laden played their roles to push the world toward greater peace, to make us aware of our oneness and our desire to evolve past violence.

We must recognize that we are responsible not only for our own evolution but how evolution continues to unfold on our planet. If we learn to cooperate—**align our self-interests with the well-being of all others and the Earth**—together we can create heaven on earth.

CHARLOTTE F. LEHECKA, PHD

Core Teaching Three: Our thoughts are our creative power.

Thoughts held in mind produce after their kind. This is the Law of Mind Action which we will examine in more detail in Chapter Two. What it means is that our bodies and our life circumstances are faithful renditions of the consistent and persistent ideas in our minds. That is why many new thought traditions have the saying: "Change your thinking; change your life."

In Chapter Three, we go into detail about the roles of the subconscious, the conscious and the superconscious mind in creating our reality. But for now, just know that the subconscious is where our real beliefs and emotions reside. We can try to fool ourselves, but the Reality is that every deep-seated conviction, expectation, and emotion is going to eventually manifest as our reality. So, if we want to know what our beliefs truly are, we only need take a look at our current state of affairs. Reality never lies.

That thought is both scary and empowering. What I have learned is that when I simply look at my current situation without judgment, I open myself to the realm of all possibilities and I am free to choose another one—one more to my liking!!! However, as long as my ego stays mired down in resisting what is actually happening, my higher consciousness, my I AM, is not free to inspire a different reality.

We are like magnets. So you might be wondering: "If my thoughts and feelings create my world, does that mean I had been thinking 'car crash', before I had that accident?" "Or does this mean I've been dwelling on cancer?" The answer to each of these questions is "yes" and "no". Our thoughts and feelings send out a certain vibration into the universe and we attract to ourselves those situations that are a vibrational match. So, while I may not have been dwelling on cancer, research has shown that there is a correlation between resentful thinking and the appearance of cancer in one's body. In Chapter Six we explore the impact of our thoughts on our physical health in a lot more detail.

Fortunately, once these situations do come into our lives, we have absolute control over our reactions to them. If we look at the Law of Mind Action from a much higher perspective, then we are able to see that no matter what comes our way, if God is good and everywhere present, God is in this situation too and God takes everything and turns it into good for that is all God knows. God knows only unconditional love and sees only perfection. And we are not talking about a God out there, but rather the God within you. That God, your spiritual essence, is able to rise above any situation and see its perfection. Sometimes, that may take a while, so in the meantime, it is our faith that makes us whole.

When we align our consciousness with the Christ consciousness (a state of consciousness in which a person experiences unity with the Divine as did Jesus and other great spiritual masters), we are able to see the world through the lens of unconditional love. However, when we allow ourselves to wander away from this single vision, then we "see double", that is, we see both good and evil.

Thinking un-God-like, i.e. unloving thoughts, causes us to look at the world through clouded lenses. This fearful state of mind bogs us down in doubt, uncertainty, worry and inharmony. When we seem to be helplessly lost in the troubles of our world, which strangely enough, we ourselves created by our own negative thinking; when we see trouble and discord about us instead of living in an ocean of love and abundance in which we cannot fail, we are reminded—once again—what amazing power we human beings have! For as we have learned from Core Teachings One and Two, that spirit which is in Jesus also resides in us.

So to reiterate: Core Teaching Three says: "Our thoughts, feelings and beliefs have the power to create our reality." According to Quantum science, every possible outcome already exists in potential, but we draw to us our "particular outcome" based on what we currently believe. This is why metaphysicians emphasize positive thinking. Because we live in a Universe where our thoughts—conscious or unconscious—-trigger the events in our lives.

We choose moment by moment what happens to us and for us. And we choose with our focus. With focused intention, we can bring about new realities in our world. Yet, it's still not so simple as that. More recently, we have learned that "feeling" has more to do with creating our experience than thought. So, the key to changing our reality is 1) paying attention to our thoughts and 2) choosing to align both our thoughts and our emotions with a new vision.

If we look to Jesus as our Wayshower, then we know what we must do. We must keep our hearts and minds singularly focused on his words: "...Love the Lord your God with all your heart, with all your soul, with all your strength and with all your mind, and your neighbor as yourself." (Luke 10:27). To do this it is incumbent upon us to let go of our fear of lack, our sense of separation, our willingness to see the other as our enemy, and our need to be right. When we do this, when we release the errors of the past, we can and will find heaven within us right here and right now. And the earth on which we live will then become like the heaven within us.

In order to shed ourselves of this false understanding of reality, we need to pivot toward prayer and meditation. I know it was not until I began connecting to my essence through a daily practice of prayer and meditation that I saw major changes for the good show up in my life.

Once I understood that I was creating my reality and was ready to own up to the fact that my reality was not working very well for me in many areas of my life, I was overjoyed to learn that there was a way I could change that. So, I am truly excited to introduce you to Core Teaching Four, which is about prayer and meditation. My shorthand for understanding the distinction between the two is: **prayer is my talking to God and meditation is my listening to God**. After learning I was pretty much responsible for everything that happens in my life, I was relieved to know that there was a path to aligning my Christ spirit with Universal spirit.

Core Teaching Four: Prayer and Meditation are essential elements of the spiritual life.

Prayer

When we take the first three core teachings into account then we can appreciate that prayer forces us to find new ways to describe the Divine, our relationship to It and our role in creation. I remember vividly how frustrated I felt in the beginning when I attempted to pray. I was so accustomed to petitioning Daddy God for help, and yet intellectually I now understood that it wasn't God making things happen or not happen or keeping me safe, but rather I was the one deciding what showed up in my life by where I focused my attention and what I was open to receiving. For a while, since I didn't want to screw this praying thing up, I actually didn't pray at all. I was stymied—knowing that my old way of praying wasn't what I wanted and yet not fully understanding how to pray in a new way. This idea that God was not a someone, but rather a benevolent force that always says "yes" to all of my requests was quite new to me.

Jesus taught us that whatever we ask for in prayer believing, we will receive (Matthew 21:22). So, imagine that God as Infinite Source is like the radio waves that encircle our earth. Those waves are always there, but it is necessary for us to turn the radio on to the channel we want to get the results we desire. God as Infinite Source provides everyone with everything. As it says in the scriptures, God made the rain to fall upon everyone (Matthew 5:45). God did not single some people out and say— "Well, since you've behaved, I will send rain to you, but since you haven't behaved, you get no rain." No, the rain goes to everyone. Whatever we need or want already exists for us. It is ours to claim.

In affirmative prayer, we are remembering who we truly are as expressions of the eternal life force on Earth. Everything we could ever want is already possible and available to us. We only have to ask. Asking is not begging as many of us were taught. It is focusing our thoughts, our intentions. The process of affirmative prayer begins with a shift in consciousness. It is praying from a consciousness of God, from the Higher Self that is in constant contact with the Divine. Affirmative prayer is the time we take to focus, to align ourselves with the Divine and affirm that whatever we need is already ours. We are simply affirming its availability and our willingness to accept our good.

Since we know our words powered by our emotions are powerful, it's important to remember to ask for what we want, not what we don't want. Sometimes, before formulating my affirmation, I find it helpful to take a moment to be clear about what it is I don't want. With that information, I can then construct an affirmative prayer that captures fully what it is **I do** want.

Often we have believed we can affect things by dealing with what is out there, but the truth is that life does not go from outward inward, but rather, from inward outward. It's like there are two creations: the first one is in our minds and hearts and the second one is in the manifest world. That is why we are **called upon to <u>not</u> give energy to what is in front of us but rather what is inside of us**. "What is it we are wanting to express?"

The specific words used in affirmative prayer are not as important as the intention to claim what already exists in the realm of possibilities. We call it forth and give thanks for it in advance. We see the people or situation from the other side, through the eyes of Source.

When we pray we become still enough to feel the Presence that is always within and around us and to know the sea of love in which we live. Prayer is not about us beseeching God for something. It is about us refreshing and realigning our minds and hearts with the Divine Presence within us. As we move from ego to soul and contact the Christ light within us, we begin to live again from our best selves. Through affirmative prayer we are simply calling forth that which is already ours.

I'd like to back up a minute to make something really, really clear. In point of fact, we are a walking, talking prayer. Every thought, every feeling, every utterance we make is actually a prayer. The difference is that with affirmative prayer we are taking the time to align our thoughts, feelings and words with our highest good. At other times, that is not always the case which is why our lives don't always look the way we would like for them to, but they <u>do</u> reflect where we are vibrationally at every moment

Although we know intellectually that every possibility already exists in the Quantum field, why is it that we sometimes don't get what we are asking for? Because no matter what we are "asking" for, we get what we are vibrationally in alignment with. If prayer seems to go unanswered, it is not a decision on God's part to deny us. It is rather that we are attracting from an unconscious deeper desire or we are blocking our good by our deep-seated feelings of doubt, fear and unworthiness. Often our thoughts are going in one direction and our feelings in another. Our results reflect this deeper truth.

Simply stated, the purpose of prayer is to move us into a state of allowing and non-resistance. We don't receive an answer to prayer so much as we let the answer into our lives. So, if there are things in our lives which need a new direction, know that we are creating our tomorrow with the thoughts and emotions of today. That is why prayer in conjunction with meditation is so important.

Meditation

In the beginning of this section, I made the statement that prayer is us talking to God, and meditation is our listening to God. It is in the Silence we meet God. Jesus left us with very specific instructions about how to enter into the Silence. He told us to go into a room and close the door, (Mathew 6:6) which translated means go into a place where there is only you—you and your God—and shut out all the clamor of outer things, including our own thoughts. This is an inner space, an internal and very personal place of total silence, which no one else can ever enter or disturb. It is the place where in a very real way we "connect" with our Higher Self, the God within us.

Spending time each day in this secret place of stillness may be the most rewarding thing we can do to further our journey toward wholeness. It's well and good to talk and learn about our spiritual nature—but that in itself is not enough. We must experience our spirituality, feel our oneness with the One, sense the comfort and guidance which is a by-product of spending time in the Silence.

How many of you have had the frustrating experience of trying to get something in edgewise with someone who talks non-stop? This holds true for God too. God is always ready to communicate with us. All the guidance and inspiration and divine ideas we could ever possibly want are awaiting us.

Our quiet times become an open door through which to experience a larger sense of self. Things just automatically fall into better perspective after I sit in the Silence. In the stillness of the Silence, we are able to move beyond the intellectual mind into the realm of spiritual "knowing". Since the intellectual mind is not capable of entering into this realm, we find ourselves immersed solely in the perfection that is God. No matter what's going on in the outside world, when we enter into the Silence, we find ourselves in an unchangeable refuge of safety and tranquility.

The Silence is a holy time within the body temple, a time of reverence, joy and thanksgiving deep within our souls. It is a time of restoration. We come away from it renewed in body and mind—harmonized, revitalized, illumined and at peace with ourselves and our world. The Life-Force is always waiting to hold communion with us. It is during the Silence that the contact is made.

It has been my experience that spending time in the Silence each day is simply rewarding in and of itself. Often times there are bonuses when during or shortly after my time in the Silence, I get insights and experience breakthroughs where I was feeling stuck. Before I took up the practice of meditation, I found I could not trust my decisions—that I often made poor choices. I soon learned I could trust the insights I receive as a result of my time in meditation and when I act upon that inspiration, I experience wonderfully, harmonious results—not some of the time, but every time!

So, let us turn our attention now to the last of the five core teachings which I like to refer to as "inspired" action.

Core Teaching Five: We must live the Truth we know.

As the great scholar Nietzsche once said, "To know the truth is easy. To serve the truth? Ah, to serve the truth is another matter entirely." But if we truly believe these core teachings, then we have no choice but to live by them and put them to practical use daily, hourly, even minute by minute. Otherwise, what possible good are they?

The four previous core teachings have led us to this moment. They have all been about shifting our consciousness first, so that when we do take action, it is "inspired" action guided by our inner knowing. We consciously choose to come from a place of kindness and compassion in all the choices we make. We ask ourselves: "How do I apply the core teachings in this situation?" And then we wait in the Silence for guidance.

But you might say: "Some situations call for immediate action, immediate decisions." Well, maybe "yes", maybe "no". Even in those situations we still have time, time to check in with our center. My way of doing that is to take a deep breath, fill my heart with love and then say or do whatever I need to do out of that heart space. And sometimes, after checking in with my heart space, I discover that I actually need not do or say anything at that moment and maybe not ever!!! I do know that any action that feels forced, impulsive or emotional is likely not to be coming from my Higher Self. So, once again, my action in this moment is to notice. Notice what I'm feeling: "Am I coming from a calm space or am I feeling angry and coming from a 'I'm right, you're wrong' space?"

There have been a couple of occasions in my life when I found it necessary to take a strong, firm stand—kind of behaving like Jesus did when he ran the merchants from the temple. For many years, that scene in the Bible really, really bothered me because I had given "anger" a bad rap. These two occasions in my own experience showed me, however, that one can take a strong, firm stance and that this stance—while it may not look that way to outside observers—can actually be a "God-inspired" action. How do you know? Acting from our inner truth usually brings a reassuring sense of being on the right track even when others object.

CHARLOTTE F. LEHECKA, PHD

Unfortunately, when it comes to taking action, there are no set formulas. Each of us is unique and we each came to Earth with a different purpose and path. Even though we may attract similar experiences into our lives based on our goals and purposes, our actions might be quite different. We each hold a different mix of consciousness, so we each attract different people and events into our lives and make different choices of action. The only guideline is to choose whatever keeps us in positive vibration. How do we know when we're in that vibration? The shorthand answer, according to Abraham Hicks, is: "Good feels good, bad feels bad" (4).

When we do, say or think things that feel good, we have a feeling of gratitude and contentment. We feel all is right with the world, no matter what the appearance. We are more aware of our connection to our divinity. When we are making ourselves feel bad through our words, actions or negative thoughts, our negative feelings let us know we are disconnected from our truth.

Putting truth into action starts as an inside job. If I want peace in the world, it requires me to be peaceful in my daily interactions with others. We know from Core Teaching Three that what we focus on expands. That means we can "live the truth" merely by focusing. Focus on peace and harmony when we're in the grocery store line, when we are out driving, in our workspace, in our homes. Simply notice: "Did my mind-set make a positive difference?"

At the same time, it's also important to recognize our actions not only impact those in our immediate environment, but because we are all interconnected at the level of Spirit, our thoughts and actions actually contribute to the whole of life. Emily Cady in her book, *Lessons in Truth*, has written: "If we have the courage to persist in seeing only God in it all, even 'human wrath' shall be turned to our advantage." (5) Remembering this truth reminds us that rather than fighting against whatever we dislike, we can either simply withdraw our energy from it or determine what it is we want and put our energy there.

It's important to remember that an energy shift always precedes a physical shift. The abolition of slavery was the result of a shift in collective consciousness. The green movement of today is also the result of a shift in the collective consciousness. You are perhaps familiar with the story of the hundredth monkey syndrome which purports that when a tipping point in awareness is reached, then outward, physical change begins to happen.

As we have also seen when our collective consciousness is focused on fear, greed, and power, we can create wars or epidemics such as the one we are experiencing across the world right now. Living the truth is very often a swim upstream. It is staying healthy despite the bombardment of television commercials about disease. It is feeling prosperous no matter what the economic news. It is staying active regardless of society's expectation for aging. It is loving others despite daily examples of inhumanity.

Living the truth we know—that every person, place or thing is an expression of God, the Good and that we create our own experience—flies in the face of mass consciousness. So, I ask you: "Which feels better: Believing we are going to hell in a hand basket or believing we have within us all we need to create a more beautiful, loving world?"

Living the truth will take as many forms as there are people on earth. Some will look very busy taking action. Some won't. What truly matters is what's going on in our hearts and minds, and we can never tell by looking. Each one of us is creating our experience according to our souls' path, our levels of awareness and our inspired action. Our vibrations—our every thought and feeling—contribute to the One Mind, which means every thought, every feeling, every action becomes part of the whole, forever.

Practice One: Listening to the Still, Small Voice Within

To be able to accept guidance from my inner essence, I first had to learn to listen. I had to learn to quiet the "monkey mind" and open myself up to receiving inspiration and guidance. There are many different ways one can go about quieting the mind. Some books suggest staring at a candle flame; others suggest saying a "mantra" that has been created especially for you. There are even such things as walking meditations or maybe you've heard of the runner's high—that place runners go to get in the zone. In this book, I am going to describe a simple technique and invite you to practice it throughout the duration of this reading. It really doesn't matter too much which technique you use or if you use no technique at all. The important **thing** is to **practice something.** And why? Because meditation in some form quiets the mind and allows us to tune into our true essence. Even a few minutes a day will make a difference. I promise!!!

Have you ever been in a conversation with a friend and you wanted to make a point but you couldn't get a word in edgewise? Do you remember how frustrated you felt? Perhaps you can imagine how your essence voice feels. It is forever ready to communicate with you. All the guidance and inspiration we could ever possibly want or need is there for us. But in order to receive, we must be in a receptive state of mind, quiet and still.

To hear that still, small voice within, we must first learn to listen. Listen, so that our essence can talk to us, guide us. And the place to start is through a daily meditation practice.

Quieting the Mind Technique

This particular technique was developed by James Finley and is described in Chapter 2 of his book: *Christian Meditation: Experiencing the Presence of God.* [6] What follows is my interpretation of his words.

Meditation—What? When? Where? How?

What?

Meditation is the conscious direction of one's attention to the inner self.

You begin by relaxing your body and then turning your mind inward—resting in the absolute sense of your oneness with all of creation.

When?

Regularity is the key to meaningful meditation. Try to meditate at the same time each day. Avoid meditation when you are hungry or drowsy as these two states are both counter-productive to entering into the Silence

Choose a time to meditate when you can relax and remove yourself from distractions. Allow enough time so that you are not feeling pressured. End your time in the Silence because you are finished, not because you have an appointment nagging in the back of your mind.

Where?

The best place to meditate is the place you feel best! Where do you feel the most comfortable? Is it quiet? Is it practical to meditate there? If so, you have found your place. It may be a room in your house, or a comfortable chair or a favorite outdoor spot. You will find the right place for your quiet time. The main thing to keep in mind is that it should be as free from activity and noise as possible.

Regularity and consistency apply to location as well as to time. Do your best to meditate in the same place. After a short time, you will notice that just walking into that space prepares you for the Silence.

How?

As I mentioned earlier, there are many different meditation techniques. Perhaps you already have one you practice or have heard of one you think would work well for you. Then, by all means try it. If you have never meditated or are not completely happy with your present technique, the following suggestions might help you.

The Preparation:

1. Approach your time of meditation with joy and a positive attitude. Have a gentle sense of expectancy, knowing that your good awaits you. Look forward to resting in the quiet world within you.

2. Be sure any jewelry or clothing is not restricting.
3. Sit in a comfortable chair. (It is not wise to lie down as this is often too much of a cue to sleep.)

The Experience:

4. Our mental activity and curiosity are our most extraordinary assets in the pursuit of knowledge. But this same asset can become a liability when our intent is to keep our minds quiet enough to listen. One way to shut down the "monkey mind" to which I referred earlier is to find something on which to dwell. That "something" could be internally listening to a sound or a word or paying close attention to your breath. Some people feel comfortable dwelling on the phrase "I AM", internally saying" I" as they inhale and "AM" as they exhale.

   A good way to begin a meditation is by concentrating on your breathing. Just focus on your breath and follow it as you gently inhale and exhale. When you feel you are ready to turn your attention inward, take three slow deep breaths, each one deeper than the previous. These three deep breaths will eventually act as a signal, a cue to prepare you for your meditation. After exhaling the last deep breath, switch your attention to your special phrase or word and resolutely follow it. As distractions impose themselves on your mind, gently bring your attention back to your point of focus.

   Disregard all passing thoughts. Become indifferent to them. Your mind will introduce and attempt to entertain all sorts of thoughts and feelings. Do not fight them. Just simply allow them to pass through. Keep on gently bringing yourself back to the process. Always be aware of the experience you are going through.

   Expect nothing: Do not be at all concerned with how you are doing. The more you are concerned, the less you are in the stillness. If your attention wanders, simply remember to bring it back to the process of meditation. Don't battle with your mind. Don't try to get rid of thoughts. Nonresistance is the key to success. Your tranquil awareness and focus are all that are needed. When you are finished with your meditation, return gently to full awareness. Allow yourself to savor the experience.

If you are meditating for the first time and find yourself harassed by thoughts, feelings, and especially memories, it's okay. In attempting to tame the mind to listen, you may have to go through some retraining in the beginning. But as you continue to stay with the process, you will soon see that the mind will quiet down and you will eventually experience that still, small voice within you.

Take at least twenty minutes each day to spend some time in the stillness. If that seems too long in the beginning, then, start small—say five minutes and build up to twenty. This activity is simply so important that you will quickly understand why you are encouraged to make it a lifetime activity.

Practice Two—Affirmations and Denials

Denials

Denial is a mental process for erasing from consciousness false beliefs and attitudes. Denials are not to be confused with the idea of "denial" as we traditionally think of it when we simply ignore or pretend that a particular situation or condition does not exist. We use denials in conjunction with affirmations. We do not deny, for example, that we have cancer. We deny that cancer has the power to kill us. We do not deny the power that fear has played in our life; we do deny "fear's" ability to have power in our lives. Denial, as we are using it, is a way of saying "no" to our limiting and false beliefs. They are relinquishments of mental or emotional states and are best made as a simple statement of a fact. First, we say what we don't want. Then, it's important that denials be followed immediately with an affirmation as the universe abhors a vacuum.

Examples of denials:

My fears are no longer the focus of my attention.

The belief that I am unworthy (unlovable, clumsy, stupid, etc.) no longer has power in my life.
I let go of my need to impress people.
I let go of my fear of making choices.
I release my fears of intimacy.
No one can have power over me.
My happiness is not tied up in my fantasies

Affirmations

There are certain guidelines to follow in creating affirmations. However, before we even create them, it is wise to ask ourselves some preliminary questions to determine the highest good we want to manifest for ourselves.

1) Ask within—*What do I want?* (Take this to as deep a level as possible.) For example, if your answer is: "I want a new car." Ask yourself: "Why do I want a new car?" If the answer to that question is: "So, I can go visit my sister." Ask yourself, "Why do I want to go visit my sister?" Perhaps your answer is: "I miss my sister and I want to see her." Can you see how your initial desire for a new car was not really what you wanted? What you really want is to visit your sister. Now that you are clear about your true desire, all kinds of possibilities open up as to how that desire might be met. You might take a bus, a plane or a train to visit her; you might pay for her to come to visit you, etc.

2) Ask within—*What is the "highest ideal" this will satisfy?* If we continue with the situation above, then perhaps "your highest ideal" is spending quality time with your sister.

3) Ask within—*What will I feel emotionally if this "ideal" is satisfied?* I will feel "joy" at being able to share quality time with my sister.

Based on the analogy above, we could write the following affirmation.

My sister and I spend quality time with one another.

Following are some additional examples of Affirmations. These are some I have written for myself. I find it helpful to create affirmations on small 3 by 5 cards which I decorate and put on my mirrors, my refrigerator and on the wall beside my computer which is where I spend much of my time. That way, when I take a break from my work, I look up and see the desires of my heart.

One of my affirmations reads:

I am vitally alive.
I have a healthy body.
My relationships are ALWAYS
Satisfying
Intimate
Honest
Nurturing
And work ALL of the time.
I love my work so much
That it's not work, it's play.
I have all the money I can spend.

Another one reads: *I am clearly guided in the most Truth-filled ways to think and the most effective ways to act.* The one on my refrigerator which I read, at least, once a day says:

As I pursue the desires of my heart, all I need is provided. I have the energy, the will and the clarity to accomplish that which is calling me. I let God do through me that which is mine to do.

The following are some examples of more generalized, holistic affirmations.

I am the love of God in expression.
I am perfectly loved.
It is safe to let go. Only that which I no longer need leaves my life.
I see that only good is mine.
I am strong and capable.

CHARLOTTE F. LEHECKA, PHD

I make enlightened choices.
I have the power to accomplish all good things.
I clearly see the ways in which good is coming into my life.

When writing affirmations, first think about them: Do they really fit my desires? Do I really want to commit myself to these affirmations? Affirmations can be more general as the ones above or they may be more specific. If you are writing general affirmations, then points 1-4 below apply. If you are writing specific affirmations, then be sure to adhere to all of the steps below:

1. ALWAYS write them in the present tense.
2. USE only positive words.
3. CONNECT to them emotionally.
4. EXPERIENCE them as already accomplished/fulfilled.
5. SET an intention: i.e. a date by which you want to see your affirmations realized.
6. LIMIT the number to three or four for any given period, and
7. READ them carefully, sign and date them.

The following is a sample affirmation sheet:

I, June Star, intend to see that the following circumstances have occurred by November 30, 2021.

1. I enjoy a profound empathy for people that at times seems almost telepathic.
2. At work, I operate in the "flow" all day, working in a state of harmony with my employees and customers.
3. I experience illuminations in which I feel a oneness with all of existence.
4. My entire being is balanced, vital and healthy.

Signed, June Star

Once you have completed them, put them away in a safe place. If you like, you may refer back to them from time to time, but it is not necessary.

Your mind loves a goal. Once you set a goal, it begins to do the work of bringing your desires to you. I recommend that on the same day you write your affirmation, you also make a written record of your present condition. On the due date, evaluate your progress in realizing your affirmations. For those affirmations that do not lend themselves to objective measurements, simply make a written record of where you are. If, when you reach the due date, you discover you have made little or no progress on a particular goal, ask yourself: "Was this really what I wanted for me?" If the answer is "yes", then include it when you set your next cycle of affirmations. If you decide it wasn't that important, simply drop it.

> *Ultimately, human intentionality is the most powerful evolutionary force on this planet.*

Research is showing us that contrary to beliefs that the body is a dense structure of flesh and bones, our bodies are really elegant, ethereal fields of waves within innumerable feedback circuits. Therefore, we now understand that thoughts and feelings can set off sympathetic vibrations and these vibrations connected with the power we have called "intentionality" can produce transformations in weeks, days or perhaps even minutes. As a reminder, when you use this powerful tool we call affirmations, remember to ask yourself: Is this change a healthy one? How will this change affect others in my life? And—most importantly—Do I really want this change?

To become consciously involved in an enterprise that may presage further human evolution takes courage and a sense of adventure. While—as in all adventures—there is no certainty of success, disciplined practice builds a base camp of security and support. No matter how high you climb, your practice is always there, waiting for you. I wish you much success in realizing your affirmations and strongly recommend that your final affirmation, in every case, be: *"My entire being is balanced, vital and healthy."*

TWO

GETTING TO KNOW OURSELVES— AN ON-PURPOSE LIFE

Prose

If you bring forth that which is within you,
that which is within you will save you.
If you do not bring forth that which is within you,
that which is within you will curse you.

Gospel of Thomas

When I was in high school, my mom came to me in frustration one day. She was complaining to me about my brother, Sam. He was not making the kinds of grades she knew he was capable of producing. In the course of the conversation, she commented that were it me not doing so well, she wouldn't be so upset, but his school test scores indicated that he was really smart, and his grades just simply did not reflect his capability. I don't think I really heard past the inference that I wasn't so smart. I had lots of options. I could have ignored it, refuted it or argued with it, but I didn't. I accepted that statement as the truth about me. And I allowed that thought to run my life for the next six to seven years.

As I mentioned in Chapter One, the year after I finished high school, I was an exchange student in Germany. While there I learned German really well. In fact, better than any of the other exchange students who were assigned to Germany. My spoken German was so accent free that most Germans did not realize I was not German. So, when I came back to the states and began my college studies, I chose to major in German. Why? Actually, I did really enjoy my German studies, but the main motivator was "fear"—fear of failure if I studied anything else, Because "remember", I'm not very smart.

Now, for those of you who have been to college, you know that you cannot just take German courses, you must take English, Chemistry, Math, etc. I not only did well in my German courses, but in all of these other courses too. However, my story was so strong that I would make up reasons about how I managed to get an "A" in my other classes. Anything, rather than address the idea that maybe I got good grades because I was a "capable" student. Because remember, my "story" was that I wasn't very smart. And our stories are so powerful that we don't even pay attention to the "facts" of a situation. Our stories have a way of allowing us to "twist the truth" to fit the lie we have accepted about ourselves. It wasn't until my second year in graduate school when I switched my major from German to another field and still made good grades that I began to entertain the thought that maybe the story I had sold myself wasn't altogether true.

Over the years I have come to realize that it really doesn't matter whether I am "smart" or not. What matters is that I discover the desires of my heart and follow my passions. When I do, I find the universe eager to help me fulfill my heart's desires. I have discovered that as soon as I get clear about what it is I want, things begin to happen in a way that cannot be fully explained.

The following is a quote from Henry David Thoreau which describes what I believe happens.

> If one advances confidently in the direction of his dreams, and endeavors to live the life which he has

imagined, he will meet with a success unexpected in common hours. [1]

I'd like to share an example from my life that demonstrates this principle. When I was in graduate school, I had a very dear friend who was absolutely passionate about his work. As I listened to him, I set the following intention: "Someday, I want to have work that fills me with the same kind of excitement I see in him." I said this to myself and I felt the energy of that declaration in every part of my body. I didn't really think about it much after that one-time event other than to notice that now and again, the thought might flitter across my mind and I would remember him and remember the excitement that thought generated.

It was about eight years later; I had held two jobs which I had really, really enjoyed and had just moved to the University of Houston (UH) to set up a traditional foreign language program in Continuing Education similar to the one I had worked in at Rice University.

Shortly after arriving, I was introduced to the Chair of the Spanish Department. He asked me if he might teach an Accelerated Learning (AL) Spanish class in our program as he was excited about this new teaching methodology he had recently studied and wanted a venue to practice what he had been learning. I had never heard of this teaching methodology and to be honest—-when he told me about it—with its use of music, the power of suggestion, story-telling, pretend identities, games, etc. I was highly skeptical. But, after all, he was the head of the Spanish Department, so perhaps I should give him the benefit of the doubt!!! I agreed. As soon as the class began, I had this incredible "aha" experience.

In graduate school I had studied German before changing majors and getting a degree in counseling. In my wildest dreams I had never imagined being able to integrate these two educational experiences. But, in a flash, I saw and truly understood the underlying tenets of this teaching philosophy he was modeling; it was simply good counseling techniques being applied to foreign language learning. In that moment my two disparate backgrounds came together, and I *knew* what I was supposed to do in my professional life moving forward. What still amazes me to this day about this story is that it demonstrates how absolutely "loving" our universe is. It takes everything we've ever done—even those things we did initially out of fear—like studying German—and somehow makes it all good in ways we would never imagine.

PRINCIPLE

These two stories have valuable lessons, I believe, for all of us. In the first story we learn how **our perception** of our world can color how we behave and the decisions we make. In the second story we learn the **power of intention** in shaping our world. What lessons can we learn from these two stories that will help us overcome our false perceptions of ourselves and dare to pursue the life of our dreams?

To stop the stories and to decide what we really, truly want for ourselves requires us to let go of our limiting beliefs and discover our true desires. Awareness and imagination are the tools we use. Awareness helps us become aware of our limiting beliefs and the imagination helps us envision and live into our new reality.

As we discussed in Chapter One, we must first learn to quiet the "monkey mind". It is what keeps us distant from the miracle of who we truly are. Having quieted the mind, we are then free to pay attention to what excites us and be willing to follow that thread. We do not have to know all the answers before we begin the journey, we only need to be willing to take that next step. Before we can open ourselves to possibility, however, we must become aware of how our thoughts limit us. So, let's take a second look at Core Teaching Three—*Our Perceptions Create Our Reality*—and learn how "awareness" can help us recognize the perceptions we are holding.

The Principle of Awareness: How it Sheds Light on Our Perceptions

For many of us the idea that we create our own reality can be challenging to accept. We might ask ourselves, how, if this is true, have I frequently created a life that is not to my liking? Just imagine Source, God, Spirit—choose whatever word works best for you—surrounding you—just waiting to give you every good thing. And what are you doing? You are putting up your hands and saying "no". Not literally, of course, but every time you choose to hold a limiting belief about yourself, you are metaphorically putting up a road block. We have to **choose** to accept the gifts. The key to "acceptance" is awareness. We must become aware of our limiting beliefs. We must become aware of the perceptions we hold about ourselves and others and the world.

Let's begin with a basic understanding of how our minds work. We each have three levels of mind: the subconscious, the conscious and the superconscious. And each level of mind serves the whole of who we are in specific ways:

- Subconscious—power without direction. It simply does as it is directed. Whatever is imprinted on the subconscious through our images and feelings is carried out in the minutest detail. The subconscious has no sense of humor!!!
- Conscious—sees life as it appears to be. It is what we humans take in through our five senses—sight, hearing, touch, smell and taste.
- Superconscious—is the Divine Mind within each of us. It is the vehicle through which our true destiny is shared with us from the Infinite Intelligence within us. We access it through our intuition.

Our subconscious beliefs are formed early in life. As a small child we are like sponges soaking up any and everything around us—good, bad or otherwise. If you think about children who are around people who speak two or three languages, what do they do? They speak two or three languages. It's not difficult for them; it's not even unusual. It's just simply what goes on in their environment.

Just so is it with everything else to which we are exposed. We also pick up the judgments, biases, likes and dislikes and behavior patterns of those around us—especially our primary caregivers. As children—up until about the age of seven—we are operating out of the alpha brain wave frequency most of the time. It is that frequency that allows us to absorb everything so easily. By the same token, because the brain is not completely developed, the reasoning part of the brain is not yet fully in place. And so, during this phase of life, we accept many things as real without the benefit of our rational mind being in a position to question the validity of what we are choosing to believe. Even if we have loving parents and are brought up in a protected environment, we cannot completely escape the impact upon us of our interpretation of our environment from this early age. So it's not surprising that the beliefs of others become the foundation of what we hold true about the world and ourselves.

In fact, our subconscious mind actually has a record of everything we have experienced during our lifetime. Not only does it have a record of the events themselves, it also keeps a record of every thought and emotion we were feeling during that moment in time. So, while we may come into the world with no fears, we are soon taught to fear. And we lose our innocence. As we mature, we once again begin to release fears, but this time we understand where the conditioning comes from and how to see ourselves differently. With practice we are able to say "no" to fear thoughts.

I have two practices I frequently use to help me get in touch with the beliefs that no longer serve me. One is based on the work of Byron Katie, which appeals to my left brain and the other one is an awareness practice I have pulled together from a number of sources over the years. This practice is about noticing my feelings, which appeals to my right brain way of being in the world.

Practice: Inquiry Process developed by Byron Katie

I am a lover of what is, not because I'm a spiritual person,
but because it hurts when I argue with reality.
Byron Katie

In Byron Katie's book, *Loving What Is*, she gives us some amazing tools to help us question our automatic way of thinking. She calls her process, *The Work*. We have to do the work of questioning our beliefs to determine how true they actually are. She has four questions and a turn-around she invites us to use when we find ourselves making judgments about a person or situation. She even has a specific tool—a worksheet—called *Judge your Neighbor Worksheet* that walks you through the process of questioning your beliefs. (2) I have found it immensely helpful in releasing a thought that was making me miserable.

We all have a tendency to make up stories as a way of protecting ourselves from a sense of lack of control. To do this we have to lie to ourselves. The self-questioning technique Katie discovered offers us a way out of our self-made hell. It is not, however, a one-time quick fix. It is a way of life in which we begin to notice when we are spinning a story and choose to question it. The more proficient we get in this self-examination process, the deeper we grow in our sense of self-realization. Until there comes a time when our mind automatically catches each stressful thought and stops it before it has time to create suffering.

So, what are the steps in Bryon Katie's process? As I share the questions she asks you to consider, I will give you an example from the story I shared concerning my mother and my brother. I am only going to use one example sentence, but please know that you are not limited to only one example. Write as many sentences as you can think of. Katie even recommends that you be as petty as possible!!!

They are:

1. Think of someone or some situation about which you have negative thoughts.
2. Then, using the *Judge Your Neighbor Worksheet*, a copy of which can be found at the website: www.thework.org, answer the following questions:

a. Who angers, confuses, saddens, or disappoints you and why? What is it about them that you don't like? I don't like _____ because_____.

Ex: *I don't like my mother comparing me to my brother* and *implying that I am not so capable as he because if she's right, then I may fail in life.*

b. How do you want them to change? What do you want them to do?

I want _____ (name) to_____.

Ex: *I want my mother to take back those words and talk to me about the situation without comparing me to my brother.*

c. What is it that they should or shouldn't do, be, think, or feel? What advice could you offer?

_____ (name) should/shouldn't_____.

(Several sentences are appropriate here to capture all the complaints you have).

Ex: *Mother shouldn't be comparing me to my brother. Even if she thinks it, she shouldn't be saying it to me!*

d. Do you need anything from them: What do they need to do in order for you to be happy?

I need _____ (name) to_____.

(Several sentences are appropriate here.)

Ex: *I need for my mother to recognize what she said, apologize to me and validate my intelligence.*

e. What do you think of them? Make a list.

_____(name) is_____.

(Several sentences are appropriate here.)

Ex: *Mother is thoughtless.*

f. What is it that you don't want to experience with that person again.

I don't ever want, or I refuse to _____.

Ex: *I don't want my mother to ever compare me unfavorably with my brother or anyone for that matter.*

Now, that we have determined a person or situation we want to take through the inquiry process, we will use Bryon Katie's four questions and turnaround [3] to investigate the truth of the belief that I held for some time. We will go through the questioning process for the (a) statement and the (e) statement above. But just know that you can do the inquiry process with every sentence you have written on the *Judge Your Neighbor Worksheet*. The four questions are:

1. Is it true?
2. Can you absolutely know that it's true?
3. How do you react when you think that thought?
4. Who would you be without the thought?
5. And Turn it around.

To 1) **Is it true?** *I don't like my mother comparing me to my brother* and *implying that I am not so capable as he because if she's right, then I may fail in life.*

Ask the question inwardly and wait for the answer to rise up within you. If the answer is "yes", then go to the second question.

To 2) **Can you absolutely know that it's true?** Can I absolutely know for certain that if my mother believes I am not as capable as my brother, I may fail in life? Usually, at this point, most people are no longer 100% certain that the original statement is absolutely true. But if they do believe it's true, then go to question 3.

To 3) **How do you react when you think that thought?** What is the self-talk that goes on in your head when you believe that thought? Would you say things like: "I feel sad, discouraged." Would you begin to doubt your abilities?

To 4) **Who would you be without the thought?** Quiet yourself; go inside. Imagine what it would be like if you did not have the ability to think the thought as you stand in the presence of that person or situation? How would you treat the other person differently in the same situation without the thought? How would you treat yourself differently? For example, without that thought I would not begin questioning my abilities or feel sad. I would simply continue to be a supportive listener to my mother and empathize with her feelings.

To 5) **Do the Turn-around**. Now, we are going to take that same statement and turn it around. Instead of putting my mother's name in the blank, I am going to put my name. So, a turnaround would look like this: I *compared myself to my brother* and *implied that I am not so capable as he.* The question I must now ask myself is: *Does this statement feel as true or even truer than the first statement I made about my mother.* In my case, the answer is a definite "yes".

Another turnaround might be: *My mother did not compare me to my brother or imply that I am not so capable as he.* Yet, another could be: *I did not compare myself to my brother or imply that I am not so capable as he.*

For each statement, you simply look for as many different turnarounds that you can find and then go within to see which ones feel the truest for you. Now, we are going to explore a second statement which was my response to (e) on the *Judge Your Neighbor Worksheet* above.

To 1) **Is it true?** *My mother is thoughtless.* Can I know that this is true? Well, "no". My mother was making a comment about my brother and me, but when I judged it "thoughtless" that was my interpretation of the situation. I can't really know what my mother was thinking when she said it.

To 2) **Can you absolutely know that it's true?** Can I absolutely know for certain that my mother is thoughtless. *I didn't really have to ask this question of myself since I already determined that I couldn't know what my mother was thinking in response to question No 1.*

To 3) **How do you react when you think that thought?** What is the self-talk that goes on in your head when you believe that thought? *When I think the thought that my mother is "thoughtless",* *then I feel anger and a sense of separation from her.*

To 4) **Who would you be without the thought**? *Without this thought, I would feel unconditional love and acceptance of my mother.*

To 5) **The Turn-around**. Now we are going to take that same statement and turn it around. Instead of putting my mother's name in the blank, I am going to put my name. So, a turnaround might look like this: *I am thoughtless.* When I sit with this statement, I immediately see how I am being thoughtless toward myself. Thoughtless to accept these words as truth about myself.

Another turnaround might be: *My mother is thoughtful.* Can I think of millions of times when my mother has not been thoughtless, but rather just the opposite—thoughtful—loving and caring toward me. You betcha I can. And when I think that thought my heart softens and I realize there is much "truth" in that statement for me too.

Yet another turn-around can be: *I am thoughtful.* For my mother to have this conversation with me, she must see me as someone in whom she can confide her frustrations.

One of the most remarkable things happens as you go through this process. Suddenly, your energy shifts and you no longer feel distant from the person or situation. Instead, you open up a space where unconditional love can exist. *The Work* reveals that what you think shouldn't have happened should have happened. Why? Because the reality is, it did. This doesn't mean that we condone or approve of what happened necessarily, but it does mean that we meet the situation without resistance. For as long as I stay in the "should" mindset, I am not open or available to insights, wisdom and creative solutions.

I hope you can appreciate the power of this process. It's important to remember that another's words are harmless unless we choose to believe them. It's not our thoughts that cause suffering, but rather our attachment to our thoughts. Attaching to a thought simply means accepting it as true without checking it out—i.e., without inquiring into the veracity of the thought.

Because of my years of practice with this process, I have now developed a short-hand which works well for me. Whenever I catch myself feeling any kind of stress in a situation or about a situation, I simply ask myself: *What's the story I'm making up here?*

As we become more practiced at inquiry, we actually come to appreciate that people and situations which we label as stressful are really gifts. They are signals to get our attention. To notice how we are moving from a place of at-one-ment with the universe to a place of separation. Investigating an untrue thought will always lead us back to who we truly are—LOVE expressing. Eventually, reality checking is experienced automatically, as a way of life. And the essence of who we are—peace, joy, and love— naturally expresses through us in all situations.

Practice: In-the-Moment Awareness Practice

Everything we do, say or feel is either LOVE-based or FEAR-Based. There is NO in-between. It is so important for us to be clear about that. Why? Because it is our barometer as we go through life. And there are a number of ways we can access that awareness. We can listen to the words that are coming out of our mouth. Are they fear-based or love-based? We can pay attention to our body. How am I holding my body? Am I open and receptive or am I slumped over and looking at the ground? Am I stiff and uptight? Notice your breath. Are you breathing smoothly and fluidly or are you taking, short shallow breaths? All of these are indicators of our in-the-moment perception of reality. They tell us if we are responding to our present moment interaction from a love-based or a fear-based perception of the world.

Einstein once famously said: *Everything boils down to one question: Do you believe the world is "for" you or "against" you.* If we believe the world is "for" us, then we smile a lot, are peaceful on the inside, breathe calmly, hold our body in an accepting stance and exude love. If, on the other hand, we believe the world is "against" us, we live in a perpetual fight or flight mode and our body, our words and our actions mirror that belief.

So, the key is—in the moment—notice, notice, notice. Notice what you're thinking, what you're feeling, how you're breathing, and your body stance. This noticing is a choice point for us. In the act of noticing, we have the opportunity to choose something different. We can choose to see the situation differently. We can choose to see the person/persons with whom we are interacting differently. We can apply Byron Katie's Worksheet to give us a different viewpoint. In Chapter Three, we will learn some additional tools we can use to help us detach ourselves from a situation and/or a person and respond differently than our automatic pilot response.

When we are paying attention to our body, our breathing, our words and actions, we can more easily assess the state of consciousness we are expressing. There are a number of different theories on consciousness and different words used to express the different levels of consciousness. I have chosen to use the words and definitions put forth by Paul Hasselbeck in his book, *Heart-Centered Metaphysics*. In it he describes four levels of consciousness—victim consciousness, victor consciousness, vessel consciousness and verity consciousness—and ways to determine out of which state of consciousness we are in-the-moment operating. [4]

- Victim consciousness—when I believe and feel that everything is happening TO ME
- Victor consciousness—when I believe that certain events and experiences are controlled BY ME
- Vessel Consciousness—when I believe there is a Christ Consciousness IN ME
- Verity Consciousness—when I believe God is showing up AS ME.

Each of these levels of consciousness has different belief systems and different ways of physically responding to the environment. As we become more conscious, we begin to recognize which of these four states we are in and—hopefully—the recognition alone is sufficient for us to be at choice point. Let's examine how our words, thoughts, body posture and breathing tell us where we are.

Victim Consciousness—When I am in Victim Consciousness, for the most part my life is being controlled by the subconscious tapes I accepted as real when I was a child. While it may not be true for all areas of my life, there will be those areas where I believe that the world is against me. The world –people, situations, etc.—is doing things TO ME and I have no power to change things. When I am in this state of consciousness, I go around blaming others for my conditions and circumstances. I'm thinking such thoughts as: "It's always been this way." There is no way out." "I'm trapped here forever." It's all about POOR ME. With my body posture I hang my head and stoop my shoulders. My heart aches. My breathing is slow and shallow. I feel guilty. My voice is whiny. Or, if I have moved up a rung, then I may also experience anger at the injustice of a situation and yet still believe I can't do anything to change it. In that case my body language is rigid and I'm practically holding my breath. My jaw is locked, and my chest is tense. My language is full of SHOULDS. And I am into blaming the other. The *Judge Your Neighbor Worksheet* is a perfect example to help untangle this scenario.

To evolve from victim consciousness, we must be willing to release blame of others, conditions and circumstances. As we do that, we move from victim consciousness to victor consciousness.

I shall never forget the moment when I became aware that I could no longer play victim and needed to, instead, take responsibility for my current life situation. I was participating in a book study group and we were reading a book entitled: *Radical Forgiveness: Making Room for the Miracle.* In this book, Tipping [5] describes an episode with his sister. She has come from England to visit him in Atlanta. As soon as she gets off the plane, he can tell by her body language that something is wrong. Remember, how we described the body language of a victim? In conversation with her, he soon finds out that things between her husband and her are not going well. As he listens, he begins to formulate a picture of what he believes might be going on from a radical forgiveness perspective. After listening to her describe her situation for two days, he finally decides it is time to broach the subject that something beyond the obvious is happening—something that is purposeful, divinely guided and intended for her highest good.

Having gotten her okay to suggest an alternative possibility that might be going on underneath this situation, he raised the question: "What if, beneath the drama, something of a more spiritual nature is happening? What if the dance is about your healing? What if you could see this as an opportunity to heal and grow? That would be a very different interpretation, would it not?"

He asked her questions that allowed her to get in touch with her real feelings in this situation—one of not being loved, and then he asked her if she had ever remembered having that feeling before. Amidst cathartic crying, she recalled how she had believed her father had never really loved her. When she was older, her mother had told her that she didn't think her father was capable of really loving anyone. That explanation had helped heal the wound until the day she saw her father giving his granddaughter the kind of love she had always wanted from him. At this point, she began to see herself as "unlovable" again.

Tipping, interpreting the story from a radical forgiveness viewpoint, felt that his sister's husband's outwardly strange behavior was unconsciously designed to support Jill in healing her unresolved relationship with her father. If she could see this and recognize the perfection in Jeff's behavior, she could heal her pain and Tipping was convinced that Jeff's strange behavior would also stop. To make a long story short, that is exactly what happened. Let me add an aside here: Take a moment to feel into the truth of this statement: There is perfection in the behavior we experience from everyone in our lives if we come from the stance that the universe is FOR us.

Let's continue with the story from Tipping: As a little girl his sister had felt abandoned and unloved by her Dad. Since she didn't feel love from her father, she concluded (wrongly) that there must be something wrong with her. Once she began to really believe she was unlovable and inherently not enough, that belief anchored itself in her subconscious—always in the background running her life. Subsequently, she had many other relationships with men that both mirrored and confirmed this false belief about herself. But because she did not understand that these situations had come into her life to help her uncover this misconception she held, she continued to blame others and see herself as a victim. When Tipping was able to help her see how and when she had accepted this false belief about herself, she was finally at choice. She could choose to see herself differently. And as each of us begins to recognize our false beliefs, so will we!

When I read this story, I suddenly became aware that I could no longer blame others for the circumstances of my life. Damn it! I couldn't be a victim anymore! That was a key turning point in my life that moved me from Victim Consciousness on the path to Victor Consciousness. Once we get this awareness, there is no going back! At least, not for very long and not without consciously being aware that we have devolved into victim consciousness!!! So, as we evolve from Victim Consciousness to Victor Consciousness we must give up blame and guilt.

Victor Consciousness—As we move to Victor Consciousness, we begin to feel empowered. We accept that there is a power for GOOD in the Universe greater than we are, and we can use it.

According to Paul Hasselbeck, [6] Victor Consciousness occurs when we believe we do have some ability to control the world and events around us and especially our experience of them. The key word to describe this situation is that a certain amount of my experiences are controlled BY ME. I have discovered the innate power of my mind to co-create my reality (Core Teaching Three). This state of consciousness, however, still has some victim consciousness in it as the two terms—victim and victor—are dichotomous. We can't believe in one without believing in the other!

In this Victor state of consciousness, I am in control of my life. I begin to take seriously Core Teaching Three: We attract into our lives what we predominantly think about for I now understand that my dominant thoughts, feelings and beliefs find a way to manifest in form as my experiences.

Another name for this level of consciousness might be Manifestor Consciousness. As I begin to appreciate the power of my mind to co-create my reality, my focus shifts to learning about the different spiritual laws and how putting them into practice can improve my experience of life.

I, therefore, use the Law of Mind Action or the Law of Attraction as it is sometimes called (Core Teaching Three) to improve my conditions. I feel a sense of empowerment. I stand tall with my head up, chest pressed out. I move with confidence and assurance. And I am very, very focused on my words. I have come to appreciate that words can **heal** and words can **kill**. I monitor my thoughts. I am more at peace and less likely to experience extreme highs and lows.

Whereas in Victim Consciousness, we believed it was done unto us, now we get the message loud and clear. It's just the opposite: Our thoughts become our reality. As within, so without!!! However, to evolve to the next level of consciousness beyond Victor Consciousness we must be willing to give up control and will.

Vessel Consciousness—This level of consciousness occurs when we realize there is something beyond ourselves that is greater than we are, and we choose to surrender to it. This phase is captured in the words: *Let go and let God*. This something greater is the Divine Essence that lives and breathes in us as us.

Whereas at Victor Consciousness, it was important to assert our will, now it becomes important to align our will with God's will. Ego takes a back seat to the Christ Consciousness within us. We are no longer trying to make life happen. Here, our vision shifts to that of using our time to discover and explore our spiritual connection to Source. We are asking the question: "What is mine to do?" and then trusting whatever comes up. Our practice is being a witness to our consciousness and how it is operating from moment-to-moment. Our goal is to be obedient to inner guidance and intuition. We practice non-judgment, forgiveness and compassion.

Our stance toward life is one of openness and acceptance. Our breathing is deep, fluid and smooth. We understand at a very deep level that everything in life is for us. Our physical body radiates peace and calm.

The challenge at this level of consciousness is to be willing to move past all of our fears and trust that all is well all of the time. We shift from wanting life to go our way to a desire to follow the will of the Christ spirit in us no matter where it leads. I have a quote on my bedside table I believe captures the distinction between Victor Consciousness and Vessel Consciousness. It is the shift from: "What can I do to make my life the way I want?" to "How can I be a greater expression of God?"

I spend more time in prayer, meditation, reflection, and contemplation, and less time fixing and rearranging effects. Yet, if we would move to the highest level of consciousness, Verity Consciousness, we must surrender any sense of separation from God Consciousness.

Verity Consciousness—Another name for Verity Consciousness is Unity Consciousness. This is when I come to realize there is no such thing as God or Divine *and* me. This is when I realize God IS ME. In this stage, I am experiencing well-being and joy most of the time. I understand that my life is a prayer and that I am literally praying without ceasing every minute of every day, and when I am operating from Unity Consciousness my words, my actions, and my thoughts are expressing God in Its fullness. Because I am God, I know only Oneness, only unconditional love. I say "yes" to life all of the time.

In this state, we are present to the moment. We experience a flow to our lives that does not require a lot of thinking. Our sense of time takes on a completely different meaning. It's as though time becomes irrelevant. When we are experiencing "unity" consciousness, we just simply know what to do and do it. There is this felt since of saying "yes" to every moment. I need to turn this way now and I do it or I need to call a friend and I do it. Or I think of something and it happens almost instantly. Life is full of synchronicities. We are completely connected to the present moment and the call of the present moment on our lives.

To be realistic, at any given time we seem to live in and from one of these levels of consciousness. The level of consciousness we are in most of the time is the stage we are living in and from. While living in and from a particular stage, we might temporarily jump to another level and operate in that state for a brief time. It is important that we learn not to be too hard on ourselves when slipping temporarily into lower levels of consciousness. It even happened to Jesus! On the night before his death, Jesus was clearly living in Verity Consciousness; however, he slipped into a victim consciousness state when he said, "Take this cup from me." It's important we keep this in mind as we practice unconditional love toward ourselves too.

The way I understand these different levels of consciousness, they are progressive—each one building on the understanding of the other. We each partake of the One Mind to the degree of our current capacity. Yet, even if we aren't able to actually live from a place of Oneness Consciousness in this moment, we **can** believe it into reality.

Principle: The Law of Divine Purpose

Let us now look at the second element in my story which is all about discovering our divine purpose. We each have a yearning to make a positive difference. In her book, *Active Hope: How to Face the Mess We're in without Going Crazy*, Joanna Macy says that "our dreams and visions for the future are essential for navigating through life because they give us a direction to move in." [7]

To underline the critical importance of visioning, consider that many aspects of our present reality started out as someone's dream. There was a time when women didn't have the vote, and when slave trade was seen as essential to the economy. To change something, we need to first hold it in our mind and heart and know it could be different.

Macy tells a story of an inventor who sat himself in a sound proof room for days with a pencil and pad waiting for inspiration. When it came, he would make a note and then return to his waiting. According to Macy, this story exemplifies three practices that help us catch an inspiring vision. 1) Allowing ourselves quiet moments in which to daydream opens a space into which inspiring thoughts can flow. 2) Bringing together intention and attention by creating a space that does not permit distractions. 3) Using pen and paper to capture the vision when it occurs, so it is not lost.

These three practices are the key ingredients of a guidance system that helps us find and follow the purposes that call us. The core principle here is that we do not have to just passively wait for inspiration, we can play an active role in inviting it in.

There may also be a few special times in our lifetimes when we experience such a strong intuitive pull toward a course of action that we know it to be the right thing to do. Even when the odds may seem to be against us, we feel these powerful summonings deep in our hearts and are drawn to respond. As we put our trust in a higher intelligence, we open to the support of many allies and helpers who want to lend their support too. We don't make these visions happen; we just play our part in them. To do that, we need to keep our vision strong within us. Then we can follow it wherever it leads us.

How many of you have ever seen the movie *Avatar*? In this epic adventure, the central character appears poorly equipped for the challenge he faces. We can feel that way too. But just as Jake Sully in *Avatar* experienced a transformation, we are also going to explore how we can experience a comparable transformation as we begin to see how a wider sense of self allows us to see ourselves differently and thus enhance our ability to make a difference in our world. As we allow ourselves to look at life from the perspective of our Oneness with everything, then our concern for others and nature flows naturally and easily. We feel and perceive the protection of all humans and of nature as protection of our very selves.

We don't think of it as altruism when family members or close friends need our help. It is just what we do. We view it as entirely normal. There is so much more to us than our separate self: our connected self is based on recognizing that we are a part of a much larger web of life. How we define our self-interests depends upon which dimensions of self we are identifying with at any given moment.

The philosopher Immanuel Kant makes a distinction between 'moral acts' and 'beautiful acts'. We tend to perform moral acts out of a sense of obligation or duty. We do beautiful acts when we do what is morally right because we are motivated by desire rather than duty. When our connected sense of self is well developed, we are more often drawn to beautiful acts. When asked how he handles despair, rainforest activist John Seed says: "I try to remember that it's not me, John Seed, trying to protect the rain forest. Rather I am part of the rainforest protecting itself. I am that part of the rainforest recently merged into human thinking." [8]

Just so, we are godlings recently expressing as human beings. We understand that the desire that life continue wants to express through us. When our actions are guided by this understanding of who we truly are and who we came here to be, we can discover where our deep gladness and the world's deep needs meet. For when we act in alignment with our deepest values, we experience an inner sense of rightness behind what we do. So, make a habit every day to think about some small something that you have done to contribute to our world's thrival—start with gratitude. Even the choice we have about where we place our attention is a way of making a positive difference.

Active hope is a practice. Like tai chi or gardening, it is something we do rather than have. According to Macy, there are three steps we need to take:

1. Have a clear view of reality.
2. Identify what we hope for in terms of the direction we'd like things to move or the values we'd like to see expressed, and
3. Take steps to move ourselves or our situation in that direction.

Our guiding impulse is intention; we choose what we aim to bring about. Rather than weighing our chances and proceeding only when we feel hopeful, we focus on our intention and let it be our guide. Since we each have a different take on our world and bring with us our own particular portfolio of interests, skills, and experiences, we are touched by different concerns and called to respond in different ways. The contribution each of us makes to the healing of our world is our gift of active hope. As we determine what our special calling is, we begin an amazing journey that strengthens us and deepens our aliveness.

Our first step is to have a clear view of reality. To achieve this, we must actually take a step back. Since frequently our desires originate from a place of a feeling of lack, we need to put the brakes on our enthusiasm long enough to do the inner work necessary to remove the blocks to our good.

Practice: Uncovering our Inherited Purpose

Many authors have different tools to help us determine our starting point, i.e. our current reality. The one I'm sharing with you was used in a course I took many years ago based on the work of Brad Swift, who wrote *Life on Purpose.*

In his book, Swift says: *Our lives are always being shaped by something.* [9] He contends that we are either being shaped by our inherited purpose or by our true purpose. To get in touch with our inherited purpose which is always in the background running the show when we are not living from the space of our true purpose (i.e. the story of Tipping's sister in *Radical Forgiveness*), we need to go back to our childhood. Remember we talked earlier about the fact that as small children we simply absorb whatever is going on in our environment. Not only do we absorb it, but we also react to these influences and make up stories that we then choose to believe. It's these unconscious, unquestioned stories we must now uncover.

Let's look at the characteristics of our inherited purposes. According to Swift, our inherited purposes are based in fear and leave us with some sense of "Is this all there is to life?" Our inherited purpose is our default mechanism whenever we are on automatic pilot and have lost sight of our higher purpose. Swift says: *Your inherited purpose waits in the wings for the moment you are not causing life to happen.* [10]

CHARLOTTE F. LEHECKA, PHD

Uncovering our inherited purpose is almost as important as discovering our true purpose because if we don't identify it—our inherited purpose will continue to run the show quietly in the background even after we have clarified our true purpose.

The following process can be used to identify your inherited purpose.

1. Pretend you are at a movie theater and on the screen in front of you is a movie about your life. We've all been to a movie or a documentary of someone's life. Now imagine that up on the screen is a documentary of your life—one that captures both the highs and lows of your life. Starting with your earliest memories, watch the movie of your life in sequence. At the end of the movie, your job will be to write a review of it.

2. Now, take a clean sheet of paper and draw a line down the middle of it. Turn it lengthwise and create a time line. Starting with your earliest memories, write down the pivotal turning points, large or small, that have shaped your life. Write the high points on the top of the line and the low points on the bottom of the line.

3. Using the information from steps 1 and 2, write down your movies' theme. The theme of my movie is:_____
_____.

4. Using the information from steps 1-3, state your inherited purpose. Remember, our inherited purpose is based in fear and a need to survive. For example, my inherited purpose is: *Don't rock the boat.* It is based on the fear that if I "rock the boat", I might be abandoned and left all alone. A variant of that is that I may not be liked anymore and, therefore, left all alone. So, when that tape is running, I am reluctant to speak out about something I may care deeply about for fear I will be abandoned. When I am in that state, I freeze. My thoughts become jumbled and I am either unable or unwilling to speak with clarity and conviction. I feel like a victim. My head hangs down; my shoulders slump. I am ashamed. I hold my breath.

In our next chapter, we will be exploring a spiritual tool called the Enneagram. It was this tool that helped me fully understand what my inherited purpose is. So, if after doing the above exercise, you still aren't sure if you have uncovered your inherited purpose, I recommend jumping ahead to Chapter 3 and studying the enneagram types.

Now, write down what your inherited purpose is. Think about not only the words, but how your body reacts, what you're feeling.

_____

_____.

5. Once you've gotten your inherited purpose statement, sit with it for a couple of weeks and then go back to it. Ask yourself: Is there anything I want to add? Does it fit the qualities of an inherited purpose, i.e., is it based in fear; in a need to survive; does it leave me unsatisfied and unfulfilled; is it always there running in the background when I'm operating on automatic pilot: If not, rewrite it until it does.

One of the most important lessons I have learned about my inherited purpose is that I must befriend it. Often one is tempted to want to either get rid of it—which one can't, or fix it, which one can't. In fact, the more you resist it, the more it controls you. So, the key learning about our inherited purpose is one of acceptance. For each of us, our inherited purpose is like a calling card—showing us where we need to grow and stretch ourselves. Remember, the universe is always working in our favor, so let's embrace it.

The more clearly we are able to uncover our inherited life purpose, the easier it is to recognize it in action as it begins to shape our life. That is a vitally important moment—a moment when we can choose to let our inherited purpose continue to shape our life OR make another choice.

I know my inherited purpose has been activated when I start to feel I have "no" choice in a situation. At those times, I am confined in a very small box with little room to grow. When I recognize where I am, I am finally at choice once again. I may decide that the risk is too great and do nothing, but on other occasions, I gather all my hutzpah, i.e., courage and take a risk. Every time I have been willing to take a risk, I grow—even if things still don't work out as I had hoped. Even if outwardly nothing changes, inwardly there has been a momentous explosion of excitement and joy. There is a sense of being alive and thriving!!!

Practice: Creating our Life Purpose

Now that we have determined what blocks us from living from a place of love and abundance, our next step is to determine what the desires of our heart truly are. What is our authentic life purpose? What did we come here to be, do and have? It is my belief that we actually have two life purposes: one is our cosmic life purpose and that is to be love. To ask ourselves in every situation, what would love do in this situation? To ask ourselves in every interaction, how would love respond to this person? The other is to express our unique life purpose through sharing our natural gifts and talents with others.

So often people just go through life asleep, simply going through the motions, doing what's expected of them rather than taking the time to actually determine the desires of their heart. I have a quote on my refrigerator that reads: *Don't be afraid of tomorrow. I am already there. Where God guides, God provides;* it acts as a steady reminder that it's okay—no better than okay—actually in my best interest and the interests of everyone who comes in contact with me that I act on the desires of my heart.

So how do the desires of my heart relate to my individual life purpose? And what is a life purpose anyway? Often people think their life purpose is what they are meant to do while on this earth plane. The key word is "do". But what happens if you believe that your life purpose is your job, career, or profession, and then for whatever reason, you're not able to continue your work? Or what if you believe that the primary role you play in life is your life purpose? What happens when you wake up one day and discover that your kids have flown the coop for example. Then what?

Hopefully, it is becoming clear to you that whenever we take some part of our life and conclude that it is our life purpose, we often experience a dark night of the soul when that purpose is no longer doable. But doesn't it make sense that a life purpose should be able to include all of our life—not just our work, not just some significant role, but all of our life and all that we do in our life?

Most people are asking themselves the wrong question when it comes to their life purpose. They're asking: "What is it I'm supposed to do with my life?" but the doing isn't the life purpose. The life purpose is that which shapes and gives context to the doing! Said another way, your life purpose is the overarching meaning you ascribe to life that then shapes the "doingness" of your life. The things we do in life are expressions of our life purpose. They aren't the life purpose itself. The important distinction is:

Life purpose = the context of our life that shapes what we do.

Doing, actions, projects, goals = the ways in which we express our life purpose.

Therefore a life purpose needs to be:

- **A powerful shaping force in our lives**. It should be powerful enough to shape us as we go through the many moments of our lives, doing whatever we do.
- **Long lasting and enduring**. Wouldn't you want a life purpose that could last a lifetime and beyond?
- **Flexible**. It should give us plenty of room to play and to express ourselves fully.

Many elements could contribute to the creation of a life purpose. Swift has chosen three: vision, values, and being. These three elements are very reminiscent of the kinds of statements an organization creates for itself. So, if organizations take the time and energy to determine what their vision, values and statement of being is, don't you think it's worth it for us to take the time to also determine ours? If your answer was a "yes", then read on. We have work to do!

Vision—What's possible? Each of us has a unique sense of what's possible in our own lives—with our families, our community and our world. Getting in touch with this vision of what's possible is one of the basic necessities for clarifying our life purpose.

Values—What Matters Most? Just like we have a unique vision of what's possible, we also have a unique set of core values that are an integral part of our life purpose. These values are the ones we live out of. They inform our words and our actions.

Being—This word asks the question: "Who am I"? Our "being" state is really our essential essence. It is something we are beyond what we try to be. Talk to mothers. Ask them to describe the differences they experienced in their children from the minute they were born—maybe even while they were still in the womb. These essential differences are our essence, our individualized "beingness".

Earlier I mentioned that we really have two life purposes: A universal life purpose which I call Love. This unconditional love is what binds us all together and connects us powerfully to the rest of the cosmos. When we combine it with our unique vision of what's possible in the world, our unique set of core values and our unique qualities of being, we end up with a powerful, empowering, and enduring life purpose.

This life purpose becomes the context that shapes and forms us as we go about doing all the things that make up our life. This life purpose has the power to inform all of our life—our thoughts and feelings, our decisions and choices, our speaking and actions and ultimately our results in life. There is tremendous power when all of these factors come into play in a congruent, coherent way. It is what makes living on purpose so enlivening, so exhilarating.

So, let's look at some ways we can get clarity around these three: our vision, our values and our being. Many authors have different tools they use to help us achieve clarity around our vision. And most of them ask us to first assess where we are now in our different life arenas and then challenge us to envision our most perfect life in each of these arenas. The two authors with whom I am the most familiar are: Mary Morrisey, who has created a course called *Prosperity Plus* [11] and Brad Swift, who wrote the book *Life on Purpose*. [12] I have synthesized ideas from both of them.

So let's begin. The first two questions help us uncover what our passions, our dreams for our life are. The next three questions explore our values and the final question asks us to reflect on our true essence. After having synthesized the information from all of these questions, and taken all of the information into the Silence, we will be ready to create our **divinely inspired purpose statement.**

1. **What do you love to do?** Think about those times in life when you were so caught up in what you were doing that your life just seemed to flow? Ask others who know you well when they have seen you truly excited about life, what were you doing? Go back and look at the "highs" on your time line for some hints too.

   _____

   _____

2. **If money, time, energy and talent were unlimited, what would you do with your life and who would you be?** How would you love each of the following areas in your life to look: financial, health, relationships, creative expression and spiritual? Begin each sentence around these five themes with:

   I am so happy and grateful now that (financial)...

   _____

   _____.

   I am so happy and grateful now that (health)...

   _____

   _____.

I am so happy and grateful now that (relationships)...

_____

_____.

I am so happy and grateful now that (creative expression)...

_____

_____.

I am so happy and grateful now that (spiritual life)...

_____

_____.

Now make a list of all of the things you value. Clarifying our core values is a refinement process. At first, we may have a long list of things we value. We will want to quickly sort them into three categories. The first category are those values that society, parents, teachers, etc. have told us, we should value. The second category are those values we have personally chosen. The third and most important category, however, are the core values. Let's begin to uncover our core values by asking ourselves some additional questions:

3. **Who are some people you greatly admire**? These may be celebrities, people from history, family members or friends.

   _____

   _____.

4. **What is it about these people you admire?** Is it a way of being, a set of values, or what they are up to in life? Be as specific as you can.

   _____

   _____.

5. **Make a list of all the key areas of your life,** i.e., work, family, friends, community, finances, physical well-being, physical surroundings, spiritual development, rest and relaxation, profession. Create a chart and using a scale from 1-10 with 10

being the most satisfied, ask yourself the following questions about each area:

a. How satisfied and fulfilled am I?

b. What value is this area of my life expressing?

c. What would need to change, be different for me to feel great about this area in my life?

6. **How is my beingness expressed?** It is the part of me I like most regardless of what others say. It is the part of me that I feel in my heart is the "real" me. Imagine that you can see past the body and see the spirit of a person. It may be that your essence is: "I have to do it for myself." Or it may be: "My mind likes to make connections between things." "Or I like to plan ahead and think through possibilities." Our essence is such an essential part of our "being" that often we are not even aware of it. We may think that our ability to do something is "no big deal" because it comes so natural to us. Yet, our essence is the true gift we bring to others. If you have questions about what your true essence qualities are: Go back to your childhood? Ask your family and friends? Write down your "essence" being qualities.

———————————————————————————

———————————————————————————

Creating our Divinely Inspired Life Purpose Statement: Pull together all the information you have gathered about your vision, values and being. Get quiet. Take all the information you have gathered with you into the Silence. Sit with it until you get the inspiration. Then write it down. Remember, it needs to be **a powerful shaping force in your life, long lasting, enduring and flexible.** Also, ask yourself: Is this life purpose worthy of me? Does it make me feel alive? Does it align with my core values? Does it require me to grow? Does it require help from my Higher Self to become a reality? Does it benefit others?

Below is a sample of my divinely inspired purpose statement:

My life's purpose is to help self and others live in accordance with the dictates of our Christ Consciousness. I am a catalyst for bringing about a spiritually awakened world where all people live in joyful gratitude. I am an instrument of peace in the world. I am love in action. Mine is a life that nourishes mind, body, heart and soul. It is a life of spiritual serenity, heart-felt communication and healthy, abundant living. It is an expression of self-awareness, courage and creativity.

In its briefest form, it is: My purpose is to help others be more "at cause" in their lives.

Now, write yours:

My Divinely Inspired Purpose is:

_____

_____.

My one sentence description of my Divinely Inspired Purpose is:

_____

_____.

It's time to celebrate your unique divinity. Now that you have gone through this process of shedding who you are not, it's important to take the time to celebrate your "YOUness". Celebrate even the smallest letting go of who you are not, for you are uncovering your bright light. We recognize this only as we are being our authentic selves instead of trying to be who we think we should be. As you continue to unravel more and more of the authentic you, the world will have more of you to experience—something it truly desires.

THREE

EMPOWERING RELATIONSHIPS: UNDERSTANDING THE OTHER

Prose

Owe no one anything except to love one another,
for the one who loves another has fulfilled the law.

Romans 13:8

I had a wonderful dad; he was what we often refer to as "a jack of all trades"—able to renovate our home, build furniture, fix broken cars, make clothes, cultivate a huge garden, cook, lead the boy scouts, make picture frames—and all that while co-managing a small department store with my uncle in my hometown. You name it, it seemed he could do it.

In addition, he also helped me out of many a jam by bringing my books to school when I would forget and leave them at home or make a cheerleader skirt for me in one afternoon so I would have it for the next day. I will have to admit that his bringing me my books turned out to be a double-edged sword! When I got to college I kept doing the same thing and needing the same kind of support, but—unfortunately—there was no daddy around to bring me my stuff!!! At his funeral, I got to hear many stories from townspeople whom he had also helped in one way or another.

From this story we can surmise that my father's primary love language was "being of service to others". And you can tell from my story that my father showered me with lots of love. But guess what? I have a different primary love language. Mine is "spending quality time with one another". So, while I loved my father and knew then and know now that my father truly, truly loved me, I did not "feel" it.

So, one day late in his life, I gathered up the courage to have a conversation with him and ask him if he would be willing to speak to me in my love language "quality time", and by that I mean spending time with one another—usually in conversation where each person is giving the other person their undivided attention.

In response to my request, I basically got a "no". My father told me he was just simply not able to do that for me. What's important in this interaction is to know that I had asked, and he had given me an honest, heart-felt answer. In some ways I may never be able to fully explain, that conversation was for me, the most real interaction I had ever had with my dad. In that moment, I felt loved. I didn't just know I was loved, I felt it. To this day, that conversation nourishes my spirit. But to get there, it took courage on my part too. It took me being willing to be vulnerable and ask for something I truly desired.

So, to continue my story. I left that interaction with my father wondering: "Since my father is not able to accept the love I have to give in the way I am hard-wired to give it, where else might I give the love I have to give?" And then it dawned on me how much I adored the father of a really good friend of mine. His father was now living in a nursing home about a five-hour drive from where I lived. On the grounds, they even had housing where one could stay for a nominal fee. I started going down to visit my friend's father three or four times a year and staying 2-3 days at a time.

When I initially began my visitations, he was still able--with the aid of a wheelchair—to get out and about, so we would go for walks, eat out and talk and talk and talk. I loved it and I knew he loved it. I

CHARLOTTE F. LEHECKA, PHD

would come home from these trips with my love tank so full that I just glided through my days. Best "high" I could ask for!!!

As he became weaker and bed ridden, I would bring him some of his favorite junk food and we would just talk. I purchased a life-story journal which was full of questions to ask to jog one's memory of one's life and I asked, and he answered and we talked. Each time we would visit, I would learn a little more about this amazing man's life and journal a little more. And each time I left; my love tank was again full to over-flowing. When he made his transition, I was able to give his son, my dear friend, this journal as a keepsake. When he read it, he confessed that I had gotten to know more about his father than he had.

From this example and many others, I have learned that feeling loved is not so much about receiving as giving. Most of the time self-help books are written to help us find love. They are based on the premise that what we want most in life is to be loved. While I do think that this is very important, I've actually come to the opposite conclusion. I believe we are by our very nature—givers first, not receivers and what we really want most in life is to find someone who accepts the love we have to give.

What sometimes happens is that the person to whom we wish to give love does not want to accept either the amount or the way in which we want to express that love. And we become frustrated and begin to feel sorry for ourselves and perhaps even make up stories about how unlovable we must be just like we saw in Tipping's story of his sister Jill in Chapter 2. We suffer a lot because we are under the mistaken notion that what we really want is someone to love us when—in actuality—what we really want is someone to accept the love we have to give.

We get stuck because we are unwilling to let go of our desire to get love from a particular person and become unwilling to find other avenues for expressing the love we have inside of us. The key to making a shift is to just "give love" wherever and to whomever will accept what we have to give. And there are lots and lots of people and animals who are truly willing to accept the love we have to give. The more we give—because we are naturally givers—the more love we draw to us.

I've read lots of authors who suggest we came into this world knowing our Oneness with our Source. I wouldn't know anything about that because I personally have no memories of my infancy days. What I do remember, however, was that at around the age of nine, I experienced an event which I interpreted to mean that I didn't count. This viewpoint colored my perception of my relationship to life from that day forward. And what I also know is that I am not alone. Each of us—somewhere in our childhood—buys into a lie about ourselves and the world we live in that creates a disconnect from the Truth of who we are. We disconnect from our wholeness.

And because we are such powerful creators, we begin to attract situations into our lives that only further confirm this mistaken image we have of ourselves and our world as my next two stories demonstrate.

Most of us were brought up believing that there is this special someone who will fulfill our needs and make us happy. I certainly know that was true for me. This belief led me to –as the saying goes—search for love in all the wrong places!!!

Why would I do that? Because, in addition to my belief that there was this special someone out there just for me, I also held this deep-seated mostly unconscious belief that I didn't count and was, therefore, unworthy of such a love. As a consequence, I shied away from those relationships that had the potential for deep intimacy and sought out relationships that allowed me to maintain this false belief I had about myself. At the time, of course, I didn't realize I was inviting these scenarios into my life—I only knew I was in a lot of pain and felt totally unlovable.

One such relationship was with a Catholic priest. Not having grown up Catholic or even having been around Catholics, I didn't truly understand the magnitude of their vow of celibacy. So, it was hard for me to understand how my love for him and his love for me was a "bad" thing in his eyes.

Eventually, this relationship ended, but I carried resentment and anger in my heart toward him for many years. About twenty years later, as a result of a course I had taken in which we were to examine our lives and determine where we might be harboring any unforgiveness or resentment, that relationship popped into my consciousness. Our assignment was, where possible, to contact these persons and make restitution. So, I began an internet search and found him.

When we first made contact, I learned he had left the priesthood and was married to an ex-nun. My old tape immediately kicked in and reminded me of how unworthy I was to receive love, BUT because a lot of time had passed and I had begun to understand life differently, I was able to PAUSE that button.

We continued to contact one another. We had many loving conversations in which I was able to share with him my hurt; he listened, did not become defensive and apologized for any pain he might have caused me. When he expressed remorse for having hurt me those many years ago, a huge weight lifted, and healing began to take place. Ah, I did matter after all.

As we continued to communicate with one another, he shared some of the issues he was presently having in his relationship with his wife whom he loved very much. As I listened, I could hear that the two of them did not speak each other's love language. I helped him understand what was going on and what he might do differently. He took the advice, applied it and immediately experienced a profound change in their relationship. With that, we were both complete and free to release each other to our highest good.

How many of you have ever noticed that you have relived the same relationship issues—only the name of the person changes? If you have then we have something in common. In another relationship that spanned twenty years, it just so happened that my multiple opportunities to relive the same issues were with the same person! We would be together for a while, then the same issue would come up and we would break it off. We would get back together again and go through the same process again and again.

It's amazing how our life seems to be a series of chances to change our mind. Why is it that we repeat our mistakes? We do work on ourselves; we think we've cleared everything out and then we seem to be right back facing similar problems again. Are we just backsliding? I think not.

As I look back on the different times we broke up and made up, it may have appeared to others that everything was just the same, but I knew that with each beginning and ending, I had grown and changed. I was not stepping back in the river in the same place. Then, one day I woke up. I saw how I was repeating the same pattern and what the underlying cause was. I was attracting men into my life who were unavailable so that I could have the experience of "not counting" and then being upset with them when they did not fully embrace the relationship.

So what was different from the previous experience? This time I did not need to forgive him for "what he had done to me". In fact, just the opposite happened. I experienced gratitude. I imagined that out of love for me he had agreed to come into my life to play a role that would help me uncover my false beliefs about myself. I saw that it had taken a lot of courage on his part to continue to be honest about his feelings. It would have been so much easier to just tell me what I wanted to hear—that I was important, that I was the love of his life, that I mattered more than anyone!

So, while these two relationships ended in separation, each time I learned more about letting go of the small self-image, so that my true nature could shine forth. And I have such love and gratitude for both of these men. Without their willingness to play a part in my life, I would not have learned how I was sabotaging myself. I am also grateful for the deep, deep love I have for both of them. I think that had that not been there, I might not have been willing to do the work to discover how my false beliefs about myself were getting in the way of authentic intimacy.

What does that mean on a day-to-day basis? It means that whenever I experience a person or a situation as being against me, I know it isn't true. It can't be true because God is love and I am Love. Everyone is Love. Our core essence is love. And if this is true, then it simply means that each situation I perceive to be against me is in actuality "for me" in some way. It is there to help me dismantle my limiting belief system about who I truly am.

It is wonderful when we can come to the place where we understand that there is nothing to forgive—ever! If we can see past the outward circumstances, we can truly come to accept that whatever is happening in our lives is happening to help us expose and heal our false beliefs about ourselves. I have come to know that I am not in the process of becoming spiritual; I am spiritual. I came in that way. Rather, my work is to release any and everything that stands in the way of my fully expressing my godliness in my relationship to others.

Principle

The principles at play in these three relationship stories is the Law of Giving and Receiving and the Law of Reconnecting. In the first story, we are exposed to the idea that each of us has our own special love language. Unless we are made aware of this, we go through life thinking that the way we like to give and receive love is common to everyone. In the second and third stories, we are shown once again how the untruths we accepted in our childhood can play havoc with our intimate relationships with others until we discover that our intimate others are really our teachers come to help us discover our true selves.

Most of the practices that support these two principles are anchored in learning how to let go of judgment. Judging is still something I encounter practically on a daily basis. So, it is not that it still doesn't happen to me, but what is different is that I now recognize it—I feel it in my body—and—because of the many tools I am sharing with you that have supported me on my journey to my own spiritual awakening—I am now able—most of the time—to catch myself before I act on these false perceptions and make a whole person choice instead.

It is so easy to be tempted to judge. When I forget and judge, I remind myself to practice self-acceptance, self-love too. Because I now get it that my main purpose in incarnating in this human form is to practice unconditional love—both with myself and with others! Actually, this purpose is universal; we are all called to be the avenue through which Love expresses on earth. If this sounds like a tall order, luckily, the entire Universe is at our beck and call to support us in being who we came here to be.

So often, because we don't know any better, we believe the way we experience the world is the way all people experience the world. Many of our misunderstandings with our intimate others come about because of our lack of knowledge. The following practice was developed by Gary Chapman. It's called: *The 5 Love Languages.* [1] His work literally opens our eyes, ears and our sense of touch. Suddenly we see that our loved ones frequently have a different love language from us and, if we understand their love language, we can love them in a language they recognize.

Practice: The Five Love Languages

As we explore the Law of Giving and Receiving which stated simply means that as we give, we receive, we find, as we saw in Core Teaching Three, it is an unending loop. The Five Love Languages practice helps us understand that to truly give to another such that they have a visceral experience of being loved, we must know their primary love language. All of the love languages are important and we—as human beings—can appreciate expressions of love in all five, but there is only one of these languages—sometimes two—that are critical if we are to "experience" the love the other person is wanting to communicate. I love how Chapman describes it: He talks about keeping one another's "love tank" full.

But love is a choice. We must ask ourselves: Am I willing to speak my significant others' love language when I am so full of hurt, anger and resentment over past failures? The answer to that question is essential. I personally believe we are always doing the best we know how to do at all times and if we truly knew better, we would do better. Poor choices in the past either on our part or our significant others' part or both of our parts does not have to continue into the future. We have a choice. We can apologize for the past and make a commitment to love our significant others in their love language.

We all have universal needs. One of those needs is to love and be loved. We can make a decision to love our significant others in their love language. So, what are these five love languages? They are 1) words of affirmation, 2) quality time, 3) receiving gifts, 4) acts of service, and 5) physical touch.

Words of Affirmation:

> *I can live for two months on a good compliment!*
> Mark Twain

Words of appreciation are powerful communicators of love and are best expressed in simple, straight-forward statements of affirmation. Some examples may be:

"I love how you look when you wear that suit."

"I appreciate your helping me prepare dinner."

"I love that you organize activities for us to do and that I don't have to do anything but show up."

These simple verbal compliments are not about getting our way but doing something for the well-being of the one we love. What frequently happens is that—because we've been speaking to our significant others in their love language, we have been filling their love tank. And when their love tanks are full, they naturally want to fill ours. Thus, to our amazement, we become the beneficiary of their full tanks.

Another form of verbal affirmation is words of encouragement. Perhaps you can recall a time when you were not feeling very sure of yourself and someone close to you believed in your potential and let you know it. And that vote of confidence made all the difference. It gave you the courage to move forward on a project you had been dragging your feet on. Or perhaps your partner has untapped potential in one or more areas of their life. That potential may be awaiting your encouraging words.

Kind words are also important. As we will see in Chapter 4, when we share honestly and sincerely what we are feeling without making the other wrong, kind words can be an expression of love. What we all have in common is that we want to know the other person and be known by the other person. That can only happen when we share with each other what is truly "alive" in us such as in the example of the interchange between my father and me.

When the shoe is on the other foot, and our significant other is feeling misunderstood, then we have the opportunity to listen with compassion. We can let them tell us of their hurt; seek to put ourselves in their place, see the event through their eyes and then express softly and kindly our understanding of what's alive in them. I am not saying this is easy, but when we can, it frequently shifts the energy around the event and makes it possible for the other to move into a more aligned space. I can recall a recent situation in which I was upset about something with my daughter and she just quietly listened. She did not get upset. Her demeanor was enough for me to reorient myself and shift to a kinder, more life-affirming place.

So, if there are significant others in your life for whom *words of appreciation* make all the difference in their world, remember to speak their language honestly and authentically. Look for things that you appreciate about them and let them know. If you are tempted to point out the things they don't do, take a break from that, look for and focus only on those things they do which you appreciate and let them know. Then, just pay attention. Perhaps, you will notice that they also begin doing those things you have complained about without you ever saying a word!!!

Quality Time:

Presence is the best present.

So what is meant by quality time? It means that you give someone your undivided attention. That does not mean sitting on the sofa watching TV or reading the newspaper together! It means turning the TV off and looking at each other and talking about things that are meaningful to each of you. It means taking a walk and talking while you walk or going out to eat and focusing on one another to the exclusion of everything else that may be going on—including phone calls on your cell phone. It does not mean going out together and texting or talking to someone else while you're together. It can mean, however, doing something together that the other enjoys doing and doing it wholeheartedly. The key is focused attention free of distractions of any kind. The activity is incidental. The important thing emotionally is that we are spending time together.

The language of quality time has many dialects. One of the most common is that of quality conversation. By quality conversation I mean dialogue where two individuals are sharing their experiences, thoughts, feelings and desires in a supportive context. Most individuals who complain about their significant other never talking don't really mean they literally never say a word, but rather they are not willing to reveal their thoughts and feelings. If quality conversation is your primary love language such dialogue is critical to your emotional sense of well-being.

So, just what is the language of quality conversation? It's about expressing feelings! It takes time for some of us who have spent perhaps a life time of denying our feelings to become aware that we do have an emotional nature too. If you need to learn the language of quality conversation, I suggest you begin by noting the emotions you feel away from home. Several times a day, stop and take inventory. Ask yourself: What emotions have I felt in the past several hours? Then make a list of the event and the feeling word that accompanied that event. If you are in a relationship with a person whose love language is quality conversation make a commitment to establish a daily sharing time in which each of you talks about three things that happened to you that day and how you felt about them. If you start with this daily minimum, you will find that as time passes quality conversation flows more freely between you.

Another dialect of quality time is quality activities. If asked, a person who has quality activities as their primary love language, might respond by saying that they feel most loved when they are doing things together. Things I like to do and things the other likes to do. I have a son and when I asked him what had happened in his previous relationship—how had he fallen out of love, his response was: "We didn't do things together anymore." That was a really helpful piece of information for me as his mother. Now, I'm more conscious about the time I spend with him. We don't get to spend that much time together anymore, so I want to make sure that when we do, I communicate with him in his love language. To do that, I make an effort to include quality activities. Quality activities are those activities in which one or both of us has an interest. The focus is not so much on what we are doing as why we are doing it. I want him to walk away with the feeling: "Mom cares about me. She was willing to do something with me that I enjoy, and she did it with a positive attitude!!!"

Receiving Gifts:

> *You made me feel so special when I opened your gift.*
> *I knew you had spent time, energy and effort*
> *to make sure it was awesome*
> *- and it was just that.*

In my home, I have several items sitting around in different places and every time my eye catches sight of one of them, I can feel my heart soften and a smile come upon my face. It is not so much the object I am appreciating but the remembrance of the friend who gave me that object.

My heart simply fills with gratitude. I take a moment each time and let myself experience the joy of having that person in my life.

In his research Gary Chapman was examining the cultural patterns surrounding love and marriage and found that in every culture he studied, gift-giving was a part of the love-marriage process. Based on his own research and that of other cultural anthropologists, he concluded that gift giving was another of our basic fundamental love languages.

Certainly, my own experience would tend to confirm his hypothesis. A gift is something that you can hold in your hand and say, "She was thinking of me" or "He remembered me." For mustn't you be thinking of someone to give them a gift? It doesn't matter whether the gift cost money, it's the thought that counts. Parents can certainly recall the many times their children brought them gifts when they were small.

These visual symbols of love are more important to some people than to others. If receiving gifts is my primary love language, I will be greatly moved emotionally by the gifts you have given me through the years— especially if I can see that you put some real thought into it. On the other hand, a spontaneous gift is also appreciated because it tells me you were thinking about me. For example, I have a friend who brings me rocks back from every trip he takes.

To be perfectly honest, however, gift giving is probably the love language which is least available to me. I remember reading in Dr. Chapman's book many years ago when he described how if a person had been critical of your gifts in the past and almost nothing you gave had been acceptable, then receiving gifts was most likely not their primary love language. I was able to quickly recall several times when I had been incredibly ungrateful and felt totally convicted!!! I realized immediately that receiving gifts is not my primary love language. So, when birthdays and other holidays come around, I make every effort to let others know exactly what I would like and then I am so appreciative when I see that they have listened and are willing to give me something that they know will mean a lot to me.

You might ask yourself: "How can I know what a person's love language is?" One of the main ways you can recognize if a person's primary love language is "receiving/giving" gifts is paying attention to what they do. Remember, most people have never heard about "love" languages, so they are unaware that not everyone has the same love language they do. If a person's primary love language is "gift giving', then you will find that they give others gifts. I have a daughter, for instance, who pays such close attention in conversations that if I compliment something, the next thing I know, it arrives in the mail!!!

If you have made the discovery that "gift giving" is not one of those love languages that comes naturally for you, what can you do? Having made this discovery and because you want to express love to your significant other in their love language, you step up to the challenge. Where do you begin? Make a list of all the gifts your significant other has expressed excitement about receiving through the years. The list will give you an idea of the kind of gifts your significant other enjoys receiving. Recruit others to help you if you get stuck. Don't wait for a special occasion. If receiving gifts is his/her primary love language, almost anything you give will be received as an expression of love.

A second aspect to "receiving gifts", although intangible, sometimes speaks more loudly than a gift that can be held in the hands. It is the gift of self or the gift of presence. This is especially true in crisis situations. Physical presence in the time of crisis is the most powerful gift you can give if your significant other's primary love language is receiving gifts. Your body becomes the symbol of love. Remove the body and the sense of love evaporates. However, it's also critically important that if a person's physical presence is really, really important to you, you make sure you verbalize this need. Do not expect the other to read your mind.

Acts of Service

> *You can will an act of service but you cannot will love.*
> **Anthony de Mello**

If "acts of service" is your primary love language then your love tank gets filled when your significant other does things for you that you have asked of them. Simple things like carrying out the trash or mowing the yard, walking the dog, paying the bills, washing the dishes or doing something for you that you don't like to do but needs to be done.

The key in "acts of service" is listening. What kinds of things has your partner asked you to do—perhaps over and over again? Try doing some of those things. If their primary love language is "acts of service", my guess is that you will immediately experience words of appreciation and gratitude and a feeling of love pouring from your significant other toward you.

Let me give you an example from my own life. I grew up in a household where my parents shared the chores. There was not this rigid separation of what a wife does and what a husband does that I saw in many of the families of my friends. My father cooked sometimes, he and mother would make our clothes. Dad was often responsible for seeing that us kids did our chores. They both did yard work and worked in the garden. So, when I met my first husband and we did household chores together, I felt loved.

However, soon after we were married, he quit doing all of those things. We were both in college together, but now he would come home and sit down in front of the TV and expect me to do all of the chores around the house. At one point it got so bad I refused to wash dishes. When we ran out of clean dishes, we had to go eat at McDonalds. I was mystified by this turn of events—not to mention quite angry.

Not long after that, we went to visit his parents and I got to see firsthand how his mother waited on his father hand and foot. Suddenly, I realized what was happening between us. Before our marriage, we had just done what was natural for us, but when we were married my husband's experience of the role of a wife based on his lived experiences at home kicked in. That's why his behavior suddenly changed! After we left, I shared with my husband what I had observed, and explained how I felt about the changes since our marriage. He was able to hear and we were able to re-establish our before-marriage way of working together.

Thank goodness, due to the media, people growing up today have expanded their view of what's appropriate behavior, but that does not mean that all stereotypes have been eradicated. Whatever your perceptions, chances are your significant other had different experiences growing up from you and, therefore, perceives things somewhat differently. A willingness to examine and change stereotypes is necessary to express love more effectively.

The key word is "willingness". We must remember that love is a choice and cannot be coerced. Our partners have to be willing to make changes. Sometimes it's challenging to want to make changes when we feel that all we get is criticism from our significant other. This is where learning the skills of "emotional intelligence" will serve us well. People tend to criticize the most loudly in those areas where they have the strongest emotional need. Remember: Every act is either an expression of love or a cry for love. Their criticism is simply their cry for love. When we are able to hear criticism as a cry for love, then perhaps we can take a step back and process what we are hearing differently.

We must recognize that "acts of service" are only "acts of service" when we are a willing participant. If I respond to a request as a demand and do what the other person wants from any space other than the space of love, I may have acquiesced, but it will not be an expression of love. Each of us must decide daily to love or not to love our significant other. If we choose to love, then expressing it in the way in which our partner requests will strengthen our bonds of love.

Physical Touch

Friendly touch increases gratitude by inducing communal feelings.
Claudia Simao and Beate Seibt

Our fifth love language is physical touch. While physical touch is not my primary love language, I do believe it's my second. Why do I say that? Let me share two short stories with you that I believe illustrate the importance of physical touch as a way of communicating emotional love. I belong to a spiritual community who is affectionately known as "the hugging" church. Not long after becoming a member of that church and receiving hugs all of the time, I began to notice I felt truly loved by this community and that I was also experiencing myself as a more worthwhile, loving person. After several years, our church leadership took us in another direction and suddenly "hugging" was no longer a priority. Many of us complained bitterly—and—after several years—it was, thankfully, reinstituted. That experience showed me that—for many of us—what had drawn us to this community were the hugs.

In another situation, a friend of mine of long standing was working through some emotional trauma and asked us all not to hug her. I was bereft. While I honored her request, I was aware that my love connection to her had been sorely affected. We talked about it at length to determine if we could come up with a win-win solution for both of us. We decided that "holding hands" would work. Fortunately, for me, after about a year, she was ready for physical hugs again and I was delighted to comply.

Both stories show how physical touch can make or break a relationship. Chapman writes: "With children, a slap in the face is detrimental to any person, but to those whose primary love language is touch, it is devastating. A tender hug communicates love to any child, but it shouts love to the child whose primary love language is physical touch". [2] What is true for children is also true for adults.

Most societies have some form of touch that is socially acceptable. Research has shown how important touch is for infants. Babies who are held, hugged and kissed develop healthier emotional skills than those who have been left for long periods of time without physical contact. In our society, shaking hands is a way to express social closeness; in other cultures, it's a hug and a kiss.

In an intimate relationship, the touch of love can be expressed in many ways. However, that does not mean that all touches are created equal. It's important to ask your partner what he/she experiences as a "loving" touch. Love touches can be explicit such as making love or getting a massage, but it can also be shown in other less obvious ways such as sitting close to your partner on the couch, touching legs underneath the table, holding hands when out in public. Giving your partner a hug when they come and go can also meet their need for touch or just a brief hand on their shoulder when you pass by. Making a game out of coming up with new ways and places to touch can be a fun activity. You are only limited by your imagination and the acknowledgment of the other that these expressions of love fill their love tank.

The power of touch is especially noticeable in times of crisis. Think back to the many times you have instinctively reached out to another to give them a hug when a crisis hits. Why? Because physical touch is a powerful communicator of love. And in times of crisis, more than anything, we need to feel loved. The world can seem to be coming down around us, but that hug is like a life line, especially if our primary love language is physical touch.

Now that we have explored the five different love languages, have you determined what your primary love language is, the primary love language of those closest to you? If not, here are a few tips that may help:

1. What things do you do for others to express love?
2. What things do you complain about to others?
3. What things do others do that when they do it, you feel loved?

As I mentioned earlier, most of us do not know anything about love languages, so we assume that everyone has the same needs as we do. So, just notice: If you are wanting to express love to another person, what do you do? Do you express appreciation, do you engage them in dialogue, do you give them a little present of some kind, do you help them out with something, or do you give them heart-felt hugs?

Then, also notice, after you have expressed love in one of those ways, do you feel closer to that person, more connected to them in some way? Do you also notice that you feel more alive, more giving in general, more positive about life? If you experience a sense of aliveness, of gratitude for life, then you have probably shared your love in the language that also meets your need for love.

CHARLOTTE F. LEHECKA, PHD

However, if the other person does not respond in kind, then soon your love tank will become empty and you will turn into a complainer. So, take a moment now and reflect upon those things you most complain about in relation to your significant other. What things do they not do that you wish they would do more of?

Would you give anything if they would just let you know that they appreciate the things you do for them? Do you complain because they never take time to just be with you and talk about what's really going on inside of them? Do you wish they would give you some kind of little gift that lets you know they are thinking about you? Or perhaps you've asked and asked if they would help out around the house or do some chore they promised you they would do and then didn't and you find yourself complaining about the fact that they've still not done it? Or do you feel less and less connected to your significant other and wish they would be more physically affectionate with you?

And lastly, let's look at what others do that fills your love tank. Begin to notice which of the five love languages seems to fill up your love tank giving you more energy and more zest for life. Is it words of appreciation, quality time, receiving gifts, acts of service or physical touch?

If you are still uncertain, try this exercise. Let's assume that you are struggling to decide which of the two: "physical touch" or "quality time" is your primary love language. Ask yourself, which one, if I didn't get, would impact my enjoyment of the other? If I didn't get "physical touch", would I be less willing to spend "quality time" with the other or would it be just the opposite: Because we have spent "quality time" together, I can now enjoy "physical touch" with the other? Also, I recommend purchasing Gary Chapman's book, *The 5 Love Languages*. In the back of the book, he has Love Language profiles that will help you determine what your primary love language is if you are still in doubt. In fact, the test helps determine not only your primary love language, but also which are your second and third favorite languages in descending order.

Law of Reconnection

In much of the literature, this second Law is referred to as the Law of Forgiveness, but for me that law makes the assumption that there is someone or something outside of ourselves that needs forgiving. As we saw in the last vignette above, I grew in my understanding from believing that the "other" was against me to recognizing that the "other" was for me. And if everything and everyone is "for us", then there is really nothing ever to forgive. We do, however, need to reconnect to our wholeness. For when we are coming from a place of wholeness in our interactions with others, we can see that every interaction is either an expression of love or a cry for love; and the practices we explore in this chapter are meant to help us see each interaction from a place of unconditional love.

The Law of Reconnection may seem to be making the assumption that we are somehow disconnected from our Source. The Truth is, we are never really disconnected from our Source. Core Teaching One states that God is everywhere present. Core Teaching Two reminds us that if Core Teaching One is true, then it must also be true that we are ALWAYS in God and God is ALWAYS in us. Yet, we know from Core Teaching Three we have choice. We can choose to believe we are somehow separate from our Source. When we choose to believe this, we perceive ourselves to be cut off, separated from our wholeness. We can, however, make another choice. We can choose to remove our blinders and experience our connection to Source once again. We learned from Core Teaching Four that through meditation and prayer, we can reestablish our felt sense of connection to our Source. And finally, Core Teaching Five asks us to take action to maintain that felt sense of connection.

There is perfection in all situations whether we are consciously aware of it or not. Anytime we make a person or situation our enemy it is our signal to go inside, heal within and raise our energetic vibration. Kate Large, in *The Game of Life Workbook*, suggests that because we live in a continually evolving world, the energies of earth are shifting. As Mother Earth evolves to a higher state of consciousness, we too must evolve. Again, we are at a place of choice. We can choose to make the shift to the new reality with

CHARLOTTE F. LEHECKA, PHD

ease and grace or make it kicking and screaming. All the chaos we are experiencing at this moment in time is a reflection of the way in which each of us as a collective is choosing to respond. Large says: "When you are able to maintain the love source vibration you initiate healing for yourself, your geographic location and as a ripple effect your healing within touches the people around you in a positive way." [3]

Rev. Gary Simmons in *I of the Storm* [4] and Rev. Jane Simmons in *I of the Storm for Teens* [5] state that Life's intention is to be, through us, the presence of God. This is our spiritual purpose. We are to be: The Way... The Truth...the Life of God. The Way is to be unconditional love, the Truth is to be a witness to the activity of God in the midst of whatever is going on and the Life means we are to be fully engaged, responsive and awake.

When we have the **willingness** to take action, then—because we have re-established our connection to our Source—we will be led to different sources of inspiration to help us maintain that connection, be it a book such as the one you have in your hands, a class, a TV show, a conversation with a friend, or a chance remark, whatever—as long as we are open to receive, the channels of input are infinite.

In the last chapter we learned how important it is to uncover our "hidden messages"—those old tapes that run our lives if we let them. We discovered how these hidden tapes which we refer to as our "inherited purpose" can keep us from expressing ourselves authentically.

Again in stories in this chapter, we are given an important reminder of how critical it is to recognize when our "old tapes" take over so we may be more "at choice" in our lives. While it's important to make friends with our "inherited" purpose and thank it for helping us survive, our goal is always to go beyond "survival" to "thrival". Therefore, in addition to getting to know ourselves, we must also learn the art of being in relationship. The beauty of our close intimate relationships is that when they work well, they can and do support us in living our lives from a place of expansiveness.

Our intimate relationships become a **spiritual path**; they help us uncover our limiting beliefs and bring them to the light for healing.

Now, we turn our attention to another powerful tool: The Enneagram—a resource I was led to that has helped me understand my own hidden tapes, and also given me an understanding of the hidden tapes that may be driving the actions of the significant others in my environment.

Practice: The Enneagram

In the first practice we saw how misunderstandings can occur because we don't understand what our love language or our significant others' love languages are. Now, we are going to learn another tool which will also help us take a step back and look at situations from a more loving perspective. There are many books which explain this practice. Most of what I share is drawn from two sources, *The Enneagram Made Easy* [6] and *The Essential Enneagram.* [7] And, I have many handouts on the subject.

This new relationship tool is called the Enneagram (pronounced Any-a-gram) which took me years to pronounce correctly! Its roots are somewhat obscure, but it is believed to have been handed down orally by the Sufis, a mystical, religious society, and introduced to the United States in the 1960s. It is a study of nine basic types of people. It explains why we behave the way we do and points to specific directions for personal growth. It has also been shown to be an amazing tool for helping us improve our relationships with family, friends and co-workers.

When our relationships are good, life is good. On the other hand, one of the things that can cause us the most pain is when communication with a beloved other, a family member or a co-worker breaks down. Have you ever lamented—I just can't seem to get through to him. Or said to yourself: "No matter what I say, she always takes it the wrong way." For most of us there is someone in our lives for whom communication is difficult. We want to have a "heart to heart" talk, but instead we end up talking "at" one another. Our attempts to communicate have an unhappily predictable outcome in which I say something, then the other person says something back—and then I think to myself: "Oh, no, here we go again!" And yet, I say the same thing for the umpteenth time anyway, hoping against hope, maybe this time will be different! But no—we go round and round and there is no connection, no understanding, and no resolution.

From our own experience, we know that positive communication leaves us feeling uplifted, relaxed, and energized, and after a negative encounter, we feel down, stressed and drained. How many of you have had this experience? Do you want to change that pattern? Good!

Because it doesn't have to be that way. This third tool, the Enneagram, will help you in three specific ways:

- Identify the Enneagram type of your significant others so that you can understand the fear driving their behavior and see the world from their perspective allowing you to better understand and accept them.
- Use the Enneagram Dos and Don'ts to help you respond positively to the unspoken needs of your significant others and avoid triggering their fears and defense mechanisms.
- Identify your own Enneagram type so that you become more aware of when you are operating out of your "inherited purpose" rather than your Christ consciousness.

From my own personal experience in using the Enneagram, what has helped me the most is that the understandings I have gleaned have allowed me not to take the things my significant others do so personally. It has given me the **gift** of being able to step back from the situation and see it differently.

So What is the Enneagram?

The Enneagram is a system of nine personality types that combine traditional wisdom and modern psychology. The system describes nine distinct and fundamentally different patterns of **thinking, feeling and acting.**

Each of the nine types is based on an explicit perceptual filter and associated driving emotional energy. These patterns determine what each pays attention to and how they direct their energy and behavior.

One idea underlying the Enneagram is that people have two important aspects—essence and personality. Our unique "essential self" cannot be confined to a number. However, what happened was that as a child, each one of us developed one of the nine patterns to protect a specific aspect of the self that felt threatened as our personality was developing. As you learn about your type, you will learn more about your original WHOLE self and also understand more about the unconscious motivation from which you operate.

Underlying each of the nine patterns is a basic proposition or belief about what we need in life for survival and satisfaction.

Discovering our type can help bring about positive change in our life. It will help change how we relate to ourselves and others as well as give us a greater understanding of the circumstances and issues facing us. It can give us powerful assistance in integrating the personal and spiritual aspects of our life.

The Enneagram is not about labeling us, but rather it is a tool that will help us become more aware of the habits of our personality that limit us. With this knowledge we can **free** ourselves from these habits. If you recall the pattern I presented in the stories at the beginning of this chapter, you will remember that I believed I didn't count and was, therefore, "afraid to rock the boat". As you read the different descriptions for each of the types, see if you are able to determine which limiting belief I bought into?

The Enneagram is a circle with nine different points. Each of these nine points is subdivided into three centers: The Heart or Feeling Center which encompasses points 2,3 and 4; the Head or Thinking Center which encompasses points 5,6 and 7; and the Gut or Instinctive Center which encompasses points 8,9, and 1. Each of these Centers has a goal. It is where each of these subsets puts their energy. It is their driving passion, so to speak.

CHARLOTTE F. LEHECKA, PHD

For the *heart or feeling* center, the goal is to **"get love"**. *Twos* get love by helping others. To help you remember their priority, I invite you to link your two index fingers together. *Threes* get love by doing. So, imagine yourself hammering something to help remember "doing". *Fours* feel they must be special, unique in some way, to get love. Imagine throwing your hands and head back in a gesture of "Here I am world, notice me!"

For the *head or thinking* center, the goal is to "**control fear**". *Fives* control fear through the safety of knowledge. Imagine yourself reading a map. *Sixes* seek relief from fear through approval of authority figures or rebelling against authority. Symbols for this enneagram type might be to make a fist or to take off running. *Sevens* shun unpleasant emotions, including fear. To get a feel for this type, imagine a fearful scene and then turning your head in the opposite direction.

For the *gut or instinctive* centers, the goal is **"power over anger"**. *Eights* express their anger; they like the truth that comes out in a fight. They may also use anger to take control of situations. To give yourself an emotional experience of this type, stand tall and point your finger as if you are saying: "Do this, do that", etc. *Nines* are out of touch with their anger; they give no credence to anger. Take your hands, make a gesture of supplication and say: "Who me, I'm not angry" as a way to experience a nine's inner emotion. *Ones* see anger as a "flaw" and attempt to hold it back. Stand tall, puff your chest out and lock your fisted hands behind your back. Now, you know what it feels like to be in the shoes of a *One*.

As we go through and learn about each of these nine personality types, we will want to learn:

1. What is the truth about us?
2. Where does our energy go?
3. What do we need to become aware of to help ourselves grow?
4. What can others do to support us?

Let's begin with the FEELING types: Type 2, Type 3 and Type 4.
Type 2—FEELING—The Helper/Giver

> *We are all here on earth to help others;*
> *what on earth the others are here for,*
> *I don't know.*
> W.H. Auden

The spiritual truth that supports Type 2 is: **Everyone's needs are equally met**. But somewhere early in life, Twos lost sight of this universal truth and began to believe they could only be loved if they were needed. The strategy that Twos developed to cope with this belief was to get their needs fulfilled by becoming "indispensable" or "everyone's best friend". The expectation is that the other will also do the same for them. Because of this strategy, the attention of the Two is focused on the moment-to-moment feelings and emotions of others, especially the people they care about and would like to have care about them.

For Twos to grow, they need to also recognize their own needs. Ask yourself what do I want, what really is important to me recognizing that even asking this question may produce anxiety since the Two has always been so other directed? Identify an unchanging self instead of the "many selves" that emerge to meet other people's needs. See through the strategy of giving to get. Learn to receive too. Notice when over giving leads to exhaustion and a desire to escape. And finally, discern when people really need you and when they don't. Translated that means: Reframe from automatically offering help and giving advice; wait until asked!!!

To support our Two friends or family members, we can help them learn to say "no". We show appreciation for the many ways they support us, but we also let them know that we do not need them to do anything for us; we simply love them because of who they are.

Here are some adjectives that capture the essence of the Type Two: caring, helpful, tuned into others' feelings, generous, likable, advice giving, and responsible. Think of friends or family whom you would use these adjectives to describe. You may find on the downside, that friends or family members who are Twos may also be over-accommodating, attempting to help or do for you when help was not solicited or desired!!! Sometimes their over solicitation can actually feel somewhat controlling.

The following are some of the ways Twos in my classes have described themselves. See if you see yourself in them. "It's almost impossible for me to accept a compliment without discounting it." Or "God forbid, if someone does something to help me. I can't just accept it and be grateful; I feel like I have to return the favor ten times over!!!" "If somebody asks for my help, there is no way I could just say 'no'; I'd have to give every reasonable explanation." "The hardest thing for me to do is ask for help. I'd rather die!!!" "I spend hours wondering if I did/said the right thing." "I can see what needs to happen in a situation and am there to fix it."

Type 3—FEELING—The Achiever/Performer

Work is more fun than fun.
Noel Coward

Although Type 3 is in the feeling triad, they actually are not very in touch with their feelings. The spiritual truth that supports Type 3 is: **Everything works and gets done naturally according to universal laws.** For the Three, the original state where things work according to universal law independent of anyone's efforts fades into the background. A Type 3 comes to believe that love comes from good performance and being successful. People are rewarded for what they do, not who they are. This is the child who says, "Wait a minute; you mean I have to be a winner to earn your love and respect?" So rather than going with the flow, and letting things work as they unfold, Threes compensate by doing and more doing.

Since the Three's greatest fear is that they will not be loved if they are not successful, their strategy becomes: gain love, recognition and acceptance through performance, doing and success. "Well then, I'll just work hard, set myself up to win and look good doing it." It's a strategy based on getting rewards.

Your focus of attention naturally goes to tasks, goals, and things to accomplish. As a Three you seek to get love and approval by achieving success, by working hard to be the best and by maintaining a good image. As a result, Threes develop a self-driving, get-ahead energy. They look for the most efficient solutions, how to be the best. Your energy goes into getting things done quickly and efficiently, in staying active and busy, and in competing and achieving recognition and credit for accomplishments. Threes are effective at promoting themselves and always like to look good.

Because Threes have a tendency to project an image of self-importance, this often replaces an honest expression of themselves. To support their personal development, a Type Three needs to 1) ask themselves: "What really matters?" and practice looking inward to find their own identity separate from success and the expectations of others, and 2) moderate their pace and let their emotions surface. As a Three, you also need to set limits and boundaries on work and allow yourself to listen and be receptive. And most importantly, a Type Three must realize that love comes from being, not from doing and having.

We can support a Type Three by encouraging them to pay attention to feelings and relationships. Since the underlying fear of a Three is: "Will you value me if I am not successful?", we need to show them we care for them for who they are, not for what they have accomplished. It's also important that we are supportive when they tell us what is really true for them and that we also let them know what is really important to us. When we see them working, working, working, we can remind them to slow down and smell the roses!!!

Some things that a Three likes about being a Three is the fact that they are optimistic, friendly and upbeat; they provide well for their families; they are able to recover quickly from setbacks and move onto the next challenge; they stay informed, are competent and able to get things to work efficiently and are excellent at being able to motivate people. What's hard about being a Three is having to put up with inefficiency and incompetence, the fear of not being successful, and always being "on".

Some expressions you might hear a Type Three say or think are: "I certainly hope I make a good impression." That guy did a good job, but I can do it better." "Why doesn't everyone work as hard as I do?" "I can't imagine going on vacation and not checking in at work the whole time I'm gone." "I need to take over this meeting. That guy is not running it effectively enough to suit me." I can't believe my friend bet me I wouldn't be able to go to my class reunion without saying anything about my accomplishments." "Why would anyone want to spend a week just sitting at a silent meditation retreat!"

Type 4—FEELING—The Romantic/Individualist

One should either be a work of art or wear a work of art.
Oscar Wilde

Of all the types, the four is the most feeling and emotional type. They want more from others and have trouble keeping boundaries. The fundamental spiritual principle for the Four is: **Everyone has a deep and complete connection to all others and all things.** Fours at an early age lost sight of this principle and came to believe that everyone experiences a painful loss to their original connections, leaving them feeling abandoned and feeling like something important is missing from their lives. They fear they have no identity or personal significance.

The Fours primary focus is finding love, meaning, and fulfillment through self-expression and deep connection. Therefore, they put their time and energy into looking for that ideal love or perfect circumstance to make them feel loved, whole and complete again. They endeavor to be a unique individual. They want to express themselves and their individuality, to create and surround themselves with beauty, to maintain certain moods and feelings, to withdraw to protect their self-image, to take care of emotional needs before attending to anything else, and to attract a "rescuer." As a result, Fours find it challenging to live in the present moment as they are always looking either to the future or the past in their search to find that ideal mate or perfect circumstance.

At their best, Fours are inspired, highly creative and self-aware; they are able to renew themselves and transform their experiences. They have a great capacity to tune into others' feelings and empathize with suffering. They are introspective, intuitive, profoundly creative, emotionally honest, humane, funny, vulnerable and emotionally strong. If unhealthy, Fours typically have problems with melancholy, self-indulgence, and self-pity. They may become depressed, alienated from self and others, blocked and emotionally paralyzed, fatigued and unable to function. They can experience self-hatred and even become self-destructive.

For Fours to grow and mature, it's important that they are able to notice when feelings come up and their attention goes to what is missing and longed for, without acting on them. It is helpful if Fours practice living in the "middle"—i.e., valuing the ordinary instead of wanting to perpetually live only in the extremes of "highs" and "lows". It's helpful to focus on what's positive in the "here and now". They also need to recognize that suffering, specialness and self-absorption are the addictive substitutes for loss and feelings of abandonment. Another key for a Four is to build appropriate action plans to keep from falling into self-absorption and to appreciate idealism separate from identifying with it.

We can support our Fours' family and friends by staying steady when Fours' feelings become intense. We can also help them recognize that feelings are not facts. Their feelings do not necessarily provide accurate information about others motivation or feelings. Help them explore the importance of reality checks. We can also help them by bringing their attention to the here and now and supporting them in finding what's good about "ordinary" life and helping them to love and value themselves. It's also helpful when we reveal our own feelings and reactions and when we let Fours know we appreciate their ultimate idealism.

If you could read a Four's mind, these are some of the things you might hear them say: "What's it all for anyway?" "When is my REAL life going to begin?" No one REALLY understands me." Why did I say the wrong thing again?" "I want to create something meaningful, deep and unique!" "Why isn't she Kathy instead of Margaret." "Oh, no, I feel an envy attack coming on!" "I always forget about it IMMEDIATELY when anyone hurts my feelings...like Carl did on Friday, November 20, 2020 at 4:14 P.M."

Type 5—THINKING—The Observer

> *For knowledge, add something every day.*
> *For wisdom...subtract.*
> Lao Tzu

The Spiritual Truth Fives lost sight of is: **There is an ample supply of knowledge and energy to meet everyone's needs.** At a very young age, Fives experienced their families as very intrusive and so chose to shut down emotionally and withdraw physically in order to feel safe. They came to believe instead that the world demands too much from people and gives them too little in return. They feared what others might want from them and learned to protect themselves from intrusive demands and being drained of their resources by becoming private and self-sufficient. They do this by limiting their desires and wants and by accumulating a lot of knowledge.

Believing that emotions are not to be trusted, Fives determined that thinking is the highest value. Therefore, they are motivated by the need to know and understand everything, to be self-sufficient, and to avoid looking foolish. Fives put their energy into observing from a detached stance, learning all there is to know about a subject and thinking and analyzing it in advance. Their life stance is one of self-containment and compartmentalization, of dampening and reducing feelings, of withdrawing, conserving energy, boundaries, and limits. They often see requests as demands. They hoard the privacy of time and space, limit dependency and desires and are good at anticipating demands. They want knowledge to explain all of life.

Strengths in a Five include scholarliness, undemanding, quietly caring, knowledgeable, inquisitive, objective, systematic, analytic, thoughtful, and dependable. They often see themselves as innovative, independent thinkers. Because they are so well-versed, Fives are often stimulating conversationalists. Fives can enjoy their own company, are good at keeping confidences and have an appreciation of simplicity. They remain calm in a crisis, but sometimes they can be withholding, non-sharing, detached, miserly with feelings and overly private.

In order to further their personal development, Fives need to learn to experience their feelings rather than detaching from them and retreating into the intellect. They must recognize that they do have the energy and support required to take action. It's also important for a Five to find ways to engage in conversation, to express themselves and to reveal personal matters. And most importantly, Fives need to practice not needing to know, trusting that the Universe will give them what they need when they need it. It's also important for a Five to recognize the importance of community. Their drive for self-sufficiency often cuts them off from essential resources and people.

We can support Fives by respecting their need for privacy and space. We want to encourage a Five to express their feelings in the here and now while respecting that oftentimes a Five may have to spend some time alone first figuring out what their feelings are before sharing them with you. It's also important for us to distinguish between their requests and their demands. We can also share our feelings with a Five as long as we do so moderately as a Five has trouble dealing with strong emotions.

So, what are the private thoughts of a Five? If you could read their minds, you might hear them thinking: "How can I get out of this meeting?" "I'm going to give her a piece of my mind—as soon as I figure out the perfect way to say it." "I can't wait to get out of here and back to my research." "God, how I hate parties and small talk." "They have not done their research; otherwise, they would know that what they're proposing makes no sense." "I really don't get why those guys who have less intelligence and technical skill than I do, always seem to get the promotions."

Type 6—THINKING—Questioner/Loyal Skeptic

I've developed a new philosophy. I only dread one day at a time.
Charles Schultz

The spiritual truth the Type Six lost sight of is: **We all have faith in ourselves, in others, and in the universe**. Early on, however, the Type Six, experienced the world as unpredictable and hazardous—a threatening place—hence people often can't trust one another. As a result the Six developed two different strategies in their search for security and predictability as a substitute for basic trust. When they take on the phobic or accommodating stance, Sixes become vigilant and questioning of everything as a means of protecting themselves from perceived threats and dangers, establishing security and avoiding harm. The other stance a Six takes is a counterphobic or challenging stance in which they decide to confront their fears.

Because of their fears that something could go wrong or be dangerous, Sixes focus their attention on logical analysis to figure things out, often playing the devil's advocate. Sometimes they can end up alienating the very people they depend upon by contradicting or opposing them.

They also put a lot of pressure upon themselves in their efforts to deal with uncertainty and insecurity. Although Sixes often have difficulty with authority, their initial response is to show respect for authority. As a consequence, most of the time, they meet their need for security by obtaining the goodwill of others, being loyal to others, and dedicating themselves to worthy causes. On the other hand, they do not like to feel cornered, controlled or pressured. When that happens, Sixes will often rebel.

How can a Type Six grow beyond the more limited version of themselves? First, by recognizing what hinders their growth such as doubt and ambivalence, wanting too much certainty, being over-controlling or protective and letting worst-case scenarios dominate their thinking. Also Sixes often do not have a lot of faith in their own decisions.

What are the strengths of a Six? As a Six, having thought through many different scenarios, they can handle crises well. They are a good judge of character and are almost always able to choose people to work with that they know can be counted on. A Six is also the best protector/defender you can get. You can count on them. Sixes hate to let someone down and even keep in touch with people they knew from their elementary, middle and high school years, not to mention college. All the thinking about what could possibly go wrong on the front end of a project permits them to be well-planned and organized.

To further their own development a Six can be and act as their own authority. They can reclaim faith in self, others and the universe. It's important for a Six to accept some uncertainty and insecurity as a natural part of life. It is helpful when a Six checks out their fears and concerns with others. Sixes should move ahead with positive action in spite of the presence of fear. It's also helpful for a Six to take up some kind of physical practice to help bring their awareness out of the head and into the body. Exercise grounds a Six and lowers their anxiety. It's also helpful for a Six to notice when they question authority rather than looking for areas of agreement. For a Six, learning to trust their gut reactions and acting on them is important. Since Sixes are often prone to creating worst case scenarios, it's important for them to counteract it in two ways: by projecting worst-case scenarios to the improbable limit so they can defuse and laugh at them, and by using the imagination to create positive options instead of just negative options. And lastly, ask friends for support. Check out solutions with them; get reality checks.

As a friend of a Type Six we can counter their doubts and fears with positive and reassuring alternatives that are realistic. We can appreciate the many gifts of a Six such as their thoughtfulness, warmth, their many good ideas, their ability to point out possible pitfalls, their sense of fairness, their loyalty and their wit. We also want to be a consistent and trustworthy person, self-disclosing our own feelings and encouraging Sixes to take action.

Some possible thoughts a six could have might sound like this: "What was that positive thought I had about this situation?" I wonder what he's thinking about my decision to help out with the PTA. I hope he will be *okay* with it." "Boy, I'm furious about that, but if I say anything, she might think less of me." "I wish I knew which way to go in this situation." "I have two pages of 'what ifs' to discuss with my boss." "Where is the safest place to sit in this restaurant?" "I need to be around some positive thinking people about now."

Type 7—THINKING—The Adventurer/Epicure/Optimist

It's a very short trip. While alive, live.
Malcolm Forbes

The spiritual principle that the Type Seven lost sight of is: **Life is a full spectrum of possibilities to be experienced freely and fully**. At a young age, the Seven came to believe instead that the world limits people, frustrates them, and causes them pain. Motivated by the need to be happy, Sevens plan enjoyable activities, contribute to the world and avoid suffering and pain.

To protect themselves from limitations and pain, Sevens seek out pleasurable activities. They also spend a lot of time imagining fascinating possible future activities they can engage in. Their goal is to experience life to its fullest, so it's important to keep options open and to live an upbeat life. Since being liked is important to a Seven, they are often high energy and both charming and disarming. Being around a Seven is to be around someone who is exuberant, fast-paced, fun-loving, spontaneous and idea- and possibility-oriented. One can often be challenged to keep up with their quick shift in topics. At their worst, Sevens can be narcissistic, impulsive, unfocused, undisciplined and rebellious.

What helps a Seven self-develop is practicing meditation to help slow down the mind and noticing when seeking pleasurable options is a response to fear of deprivation, a desire to escape responsibilities that constrain their freedom, or an escape from pain. Sevens need to practice attending to and accepting the present situation whether painful or pleasureful, stimulating or boring. Since a Seven is an option person, it's hard for them to commit, so working on one thing at a time until completion is important for a

Seven's growth. Recognizing that life is choices, it's helpful for a Seven to let go recognizing that sometimes less can be more; to practice holding their ground and resisting rationalizations when making commitments; and noticing subtle superiority stances they take as a result of their upbeat approach to life.

As friends of Sevens, we can support them in their self-development by encouraging them to make deep commitments and by providing a supportive framework for moving into painful situations. Also, since a Seven's mind is always on the move, when talking with them, apply the KISS principle. (Keep it sweet and simple!—my version!)

If you could get into the head of a Type Seven, you might find them thinking: "I have to keep my options open." "I wish she would hurry up and say what she's got to say." "I'm getting bored. I need to find something exciting to do." I hate it when I get distracted. It's hard to get back on track." "I think I'll watch TV. I'm needing a little distraction after that not so pleasant conversation with…" "I don't know why my friend thinks I'm not a good listener".

Type 8—GUT/INSTINCT—The Boss/Protector/Leader

We will either find a way…or make one.
Hannibal

The spiritual principle that Type Eight lost sight of is: **Everyone begins in innocence and can sense truth.** What Eights came to believe instead is that life is hard and unjust—a place where the powerful take advantage of others. This power is to be resisted. They are, therefore, motivated by the need to be self-reliant and strong as a way of avoiding feeling weak or dependent.

As a consequence, eights put their energy into control and dominance of their space, and inadvertently, of the people and things in their space. Because of their direct, authoritative style, others may often perceive them as confrontational, intimidating and controlling. Eights are also natural born leaders who have the ability to energize others into action, and often see themselves as protectors of the weak and innocent.

What an eight most fears is being seen as weak which they equate to being vulnerable, uncertain or dependent. For an Eight to let go of these fears they bought into as a small child, they must notice their intensity and impact on others and recognize that their attempt to control any and all situations is often a way to mask their own vulnerability. To grow and develop, it's important for an Eight to begin to value tenderness and sensitivity in themselves. They also need to practice waiting and listening before taking action as a way to moderate their own impulsivity. It's important that they learn to compromise and seek win-win solutions.

The strengths of an Eight are their courage, persistence, fairness and decisiveness. We can support them in their development by standing our ground with an Eight. We can also provide feedback about their impact on us, speak our own truth and support them when they reveal softer feelings and vulnerabilities.

If you could get into the head of an eight, here are some of the things you might hear them say or think! "I'm like a sentry whose always ready for battle at a moment's notice. It's not something I think about—just an automatic response." "I've always been the go-to guy when shit hits the fan." "I'm completely myself when I'm in battle." "Ask for help, No. I don't ask. I tell them how it's going to be." "I can chat and visit in a social activity. However, if people don't know what to do, then I would take over and tell them what to do." "I don't do emotions and I don't like others to." "I'm all or nothing. Anything else is 'half-ass'. Balance is boring!!!"

Type 9—GUT/INSTINCT—The Mediator/Peacemaker

> *It is well to remember that the entire population of the universe,*
> *with one trifling exception, is composed of others.*
> John Andrew Holmes

The fundamental truth that Nines lost sight of is: **Everyone belongs equally in a state of unconditional love and union.** Instead, they came to believe that the world makes people unimportant and the only way to feel any sense of belonging and connection is through blending in—not rocking the boat. As a consequence, Nines frequently lose sight of what's important to them in their efforts to merge with others. They put their own needs and priorities on the back burner and, instead, spend their time and energy on the agendas, requests and demands of others.

Nines will do everything they can to avoid conflict, confrontation, and feeling uncomfortable. Finding it stressful to make timely decisions and set priorities, they can often feel overwhelmed by too many competing demands on their attention and energy. As a consequence, they often find themselves procrastinating when they get around to it! As a consequence, Nines like to maintain structure and routine as a way of keeping life predictable and can often be found doing the less essential and comforting activities rather than the more important and more disturbing ones.

Although Nines have no problem recognizing positive feelings, they are challenged to recognize negative feelings—especially feelings of anger. As a Nine develops themselves spiritually, they begin to use anger as a signal to alert themselves to the fact that they are feeling resentment and anger about some life circumstance. Since it's really challenging for a Nine to figure out what they want in any given situation, the anger helps them get in touch firstly with what they don't want. From there, they can ask themselves the all-important question: "What is it that I do want for myself in this situation? It's important for a Nine to remind themselves that they are important, they do matter and that they deserve to pursue their own agenda. For a Nine to grow, they must also quit making everything equally important which causes them to miss out on their real priorities, and they must be willing to accept the discomfort and disruption required for change.

Your Nine friends have many strengths. They are attentive to others, empathic, supportive, accountable and steadfast. To support your Nine friends, encourage them to express their own position. Ask them what they want and what is good for them and then give them the time to figure out the answer. Support them when they act responsibly toward themselves and encourage them to set and keep their own boundaries, limits and priorities.

If you could be a fly on the wall, you might hear Nines say the following things: "Should I say anything or not?" "How can I let them know how I'm feeling without hurting their feelings?" "It's easy for me to know what to do for the other person, but what do I need to do for myself?" "The house just burned down. Is that any reason to get upset?" "When I hear one position, it makes sense and then when I hear the other position, it also makes sense. I just have no idea what position I should take. They all make perfect sense to me." "Thank, God for Rosenberg and his Compassionate Communication skills. Now, I finally have a safe way to express myself!" "My taxes are due tomorrow. I'll do them after I clean my desk."

Type One—GUT/INSTINCT—The Perfectionist

> *I may have many faults but being wrong isn't one of them!*
> Jimmy Hoffa

The spiritual truth that Ones lost sight of is: **We are all one and are perfect just as we are.** Early in life, the Ones came to accept another reality. They came to believe that people are not accepted for who they are. Instead, one must be "good" to receive love. Their greatest fear is "being bad", so they put their energy into being responsible, doing things the correct way, following the rules and living by high internal standards. The key word in the life of a One is "should".

As a result of the One's pre-occupation with the "rightness" and "wrongness" of a thing, they are attuned to those things in life that need to be corrected. This need for correction can also extend to the people in their lives. Ones may be prone to give others critical feedback regarding the "rightness" or "wrongness" of their behavior while at the same time being sensitive to criticism themselves. Having spent so much time and energy getting things right, Ones cannot imagine anyone could find any objections to any of the decisions or actions they take. As a consequence, while Ones can give out constructive criticism, they often resent it when anyone offers them constructive feedback.

Because of their fear of being totally unworthy of love and positive regard, they do everything they can to avoid making mistakes, losing self-control, or violating social norms. In so doing, Ones often disown their own feelings and their body and allow their desire for order and efficiency to control their lives believing that it is up to them to fix everything.

The upside of being a One is that Ones are loyal, dedicated, conscientious, and helpful. They are self-disciplined and able to accomplish a great deal. They are able to put facts together, come to good understandings and figure out wise solutions. Ones work hard to make the world a better place and at being the best they can be and bringing out the best in other people.

What a One needs to learn to help themselves is to be less hard on themselves, to spend some time each day doing some activities they enjoy even if they need to make the activity a "should" in order to be willing to let themselves do it. Avoid the word "should". Ones should change "should" sentences to "I want to… or I don't want to…" statements. It's important for Ones to take vacations to get away from work and compulsive doing. Ones believe that they "should" not get angry. It's helpful for a One, therefore, to accept anger as a normal and useful human emotion. It's also important for Ones to recognize when they are putting unrealistic expectations upon themselves or others. Ones need to learn to ask for help so that they are not doing more than their fair share of the work, and if they are concerned that the other person won't do as good a job as they would, then ask another One to do it!!! And instead of mentally rehashing past mistakes, Ones need to also remind themselves of their accomplishments. Ones! Don't let one flaw in your performance make you feel worthless; be willing, instead to forgive yourself and others for flaws and mistakes.

As a friend of a One, we can support them by encouraging them to go easy on themselves and take regular breaks from work. Help them get in touch with their sense of humor. Provide them with a non-judgmental way of seeing a situation or some character flaw they believe they have. Help them explore rigid rules and internal strictness. Also, help them to recognize that their feelings are legitimate and that they have a right to feel them.

If you could listen into a Ones self-talk, you might hear them saying: "I don't know why somebody commits to doing something if they are not going to do it right." "I should have checked the figures one more time." "I could use some help but nobody can do it as well as I can". "Am I properly dressed?" "I should have run the meeting more fairly." "I'm not sure I should take that on as I may not be able to do it well enough to suit me." "Sure, I'll come into work this weekend. I know work comes first. Pleasure can wait."

To summarize this section on the enneagram, let us imagine that taken all together, the nine enneagram types are a perfect expression of the essence of God. Each one of us when we came into this incarnation chose to learn how to fully express one of these nine essences. And as is often the case, our environment introduces us to our essence by giving us experiences of its opposite. Yet, we have also been given the opportunity to grow beyond our particular "stuckness" and learn to embody our enneagram type in its fullness—enriching the lives of others as we bring our particular insights to bear in our interactions.

As we saw in the vignettes in this chapter, we—sometimes—instead of being the "way of God" actually get "in the way of God" expressing through us. Often this happens because we see the other as our enemy rather than our friend. Those same situations would be experienced completely differently were we coming from a place of "wholeness" in our interaction with others.

The two practices introduced in this chapter have been instrumental in providing us with tools to help us heal our wounded minds and expand our ability to demonstrate compassion. There is a saying attributed to Aristotle: "Know thyself". What does it mean to know myself? Does it mean to know what my love language is? Does it mean to recognize who I am not as the enneagram helps us see? What I find helpful about having these two practices in our toolkit is that we are better able to not only know ourselves better, but also see our relationships with one another through the eyes of love. We learn to both recognize, value and appreciate each other's uniqueness. In the following chapter we are introduced to a third practice, Conscious Communication. Conscious Communication supports us in letting go of the notion that someone is against us and, instead, provides us with a way to create win/win solutions. Conscious Communication helps us stay connected to ourselves and the other in loving, nurturing ways.

I am so grateful for the work of Simmons and Tipping who helped me see that no one and no situation is ever against me and I am grateful to Rosenberg (Chapter Four) for giving me communication tools that allow me to express what is alive in me without making the other wrong.

In my work as an educator, I have known and taught that we all learn differently. We each have our own favorite way of taking in information. Some of us learn best through visuals, others from hearing and others from experiencing, so it made perfect sense to me that we might also have different "love" languages and different enneagram styles.

Each time we are gifted with new understandings, we experience more freedom. When I learned about the different love languages and the enneagram, I was gifted with even more ways of not only knowing myself and my preferences, but the preferences of others in my life too.

While there is much more we can learn, the bottom line, however, is to recognize as I have mentioned previously, every interaction is either an expression of our connectedness to Love or an expression of our disconnectedness from Love. To restore our connection, we need to tap into Source in whatever way works best for us and then be guided by the direction we get. We can always trust the guidance of Source.

Practice: Casting the Burden

There are times, however, when—even with my best intentions—I am not able to see my way to the light. Since my intention is to be the Way, the Truth and the Life of God in my relationship with others, I call on one of the most powerful tools I have in my toolbox to reconnect to Source. I refer to it as casting the burden. Burdens are fear energy. We want to cast our fear—our resistances to what is—on the Divinity within us or the Divinity in another whom we trust can help us when we are feeling as though we cannot help ourselves. When we give over our fear to our Higher Self, God, Jesus, or any other Being in whom we have confidence, we can immediately feel the burden lift.

This is my go-to when all of the other techniques I often use do not seem to be moving me out of my fear state. It's when I think to myself: "Well, maybe, I can't do anything to change this situation, but I know who can: Jesus can! Bruno Groening can!

I remind myself of all of the scriptures in which Jesus performed various miracles. More recently, I have also studied the life of Bruno Groening, a German mystic (1906-1959) who performed thousands of healing miracles during his life time. Both taught that "with God, all things are possible." I remind myself of this truth, I ask for their assistance and I release it all, give it over to them in the confidence that they are connected to Source and by extension—since we are all One, I am connected too.

I may not be in a connected enough state in the moment to re-center myself and recognize my own divinity, but I have confidence in their ability. I can call on them, having complete faith they hear me. Sometimes, it's just such a relief to know we are not alone, never alone! And with that knowing, I can let go of whatever has been weighing me down. I know that my concern is in good hands. My faith is restored. ALL IS WELL.

FOUR

INTERPERSONAL RELATIONSHIPS AND EFFECTIVE COMMUNICATION
HOW FULL IS YOUR TANK?

Prose

---

*Everyone has an invisible bucket. We are at
our best when our buckets are overflowing—
and at our worst when they are empty.
Everyone also has an invisible dipper. In each
interaction, we can use our dipper either
to fill or to dip from others' buckets.
Whenever we choose to fill others'
buckets, we in turn fill our own.*

—Tom Rath

Just recently, I was driving through Starbucks and when I went to pay, the cashier told me that the person in front of me had already paid for my food. Wow! What a gift? Then, she asked me if I would like to pay it forward too. I jumped at the chance as my bucket had just been filled!

Sometimes, if we want to get our buckets filled, we have to be willing to ask for what we want. I was in graduate school and doing my counseling internship at a half-way house in Atlanta. After each group counseling session, the instructor, who was in the group with me, would debrief the session with me. During this time, she only gave me feedback on the things I had done incorrectly. After about three months, one day I burst out: "Is there anything I do right?"

Once I blurted out the question, I began getting both positive and constructive feedback. And it was just in time too, as I was very near deciding I was obviously not cut out to be a therapist.

At this time, I had not yet been introduced to the notion that "everything is for us", but as I look back on this experience, I see what a pivotal moment it was in my life. As an educator, it taught me the importance of focusing on what students were doing right and, maybe, just maybe, giving them some feedback on needed areas of improvement. But mainly my focus has always been on looking for and supporting a person's strengths. When I do that the other areas just seem to kind of take care of themselves. I have found this to be true in every area of my life—in my relationships with my colleagues, my children, my friends—everyone.

But what does this support actually look like? It means creating individual connections, learning what's important—what would fill up the other's love bucket. It's an awesome responsibility we each have when we recognize that each moment matters. That our words have the potential to lift a person up or kill their enthusiasm. And not only do we owe it to the other person, we also owe it to ourselves to keep our own buckets full. For if our buckets are empty, how can we fill another's?

I have a special needs daughter who was living in a group home for which we had waited seven years to secure a spot. For the first few years, everything was wonderful. Then, they had a change in staff and began to bring on people who were good at doing the paperwork, but who were less skilled at interacting with the clients. Things began happening that caused my daughter a great deal of upset.

CHARLOTTE F. LEHECKA, PHD

I began interacting with the person in charge of the program and each time we interacted, things only seemed to get worse. Being a very protective mother, I was upset and asked for a meeting to discuss what was going on and what we might do about it.

The town where the group home was located is about 1 ½ hours from my home. So, on the drive down I was angrily condemning said personnel and planning my attack strategy. Then, about halfway down, it occurred to me that this was not the kind of energy I wanted to bring into this conversation. I began to immediately imagine a set of circumstances where everyone walked away from the meeting feeling good about the outcome. What a difference! I went from a heart full of judgment and condemnation to one filled with loving kindness.

There were about ten of us at the meeting—all representing different groups of people who worked with my daughter. At points along the way, the conversation did heat up and we seemed to be at a stalemate. During this time, I kept bringing myself back to my vision for the meeting and then suddenly—out of nowhere—someone from the group—a person whom you could sense didn't have an investment in this conversation beyond coming up with a solution that would be best for my daughter—offered up a suggestion that none of us had even considered before—another placement for my daughter closer to home.

I can still remember how the suggestion landed within me. At first there was shock and disbelief and then as I sat with this possibility, I felt my heart lift and excitement grow. I also sensed by looking around at the faces of the others in the group, that this suggestion was also agreeable to them.

I came back home, and her care coordinator lined up several group homes for me to visit. When I saw the name of the last one we were to visit, I thought to myself: "Wow, if this organization lives up to its name—Servant's Heart—it will be the perfect placement". As you might have guessed, it did turn out to be a great placement for my daughter who continues to live in one of their group homes and participate in their day program. And an additional bonus, she is only ten minutes away from my home!

Principle

Both of the above vignettes are examples of interactions in which I had a choice. In vignette 1, I could have continued to pretend that everything was "okay" when it was not or I could choose to let the other person know what I was feeling. In the second vignette, I also had a choice. I could go into the meeting seeing the "other" as the enemy or make a different decision. I could choose to come from a place of peace, harmony and love. I'm not sure that in either of those interactions I got there all the way, but they did spur me on to learn how to relate more effectively. With that desire came the understanding that relating with others from a place of wholeness is, indeed, a spiritual path.

Relationships as a Spiritual Path

At one time or another virtually all of us have experienced times in our lives when we just couldn't seem to get it right with our fellow human beings. Yet, our connection with others is so basic to our nature. Why, then, do we so often separate ourselves from others when touching someone soul to soul is such a beautiful and satisfying experience?

Did you know that there is a level in every human soul which knows no conflict, competition, or contempt, a level which knows only peace, harmony and love? It is the Christ essence in us, our innate divinity. On that level there is NO distinction between us and them. We are all ONE. If we but search for it, we will discover that there is a golden thread, a golden link that binds us all together. We can find it in ourselves and we can find it in others.

Every heart yearns to give and receive love. That is simply the way we are made. In the worldly dimension, we see others as different from ourselves and we make judgements about those differences. But when we are operating from our Christ Consciousness, we see others as part of ourselves. We see no boundaries.

Science even confirms our Oneness. Studies show that when we breathe in air, the molecules we take in were in someone else's body first and when we breathe out, we share our molecules with others. This constant exchange shows on the physical level how we are a part of all creation.

Is there a relationship that has you upset or frustrated or depressed? It doesn't matter if it's with a spouse, a child, an acquaintance, a relative or a friend. If you want it to improve, the method is the same: give from your Christ Consciousness. Raise yourself out of any negative emotions and reactions and become aware of the presence of God within you. It is as simple as that! It *always* works! Why? Because when we are able to raise our "giving" to the level of the Christ Consciousness, we will be dealing directly from Christ to Christ. Relating to others in this way has an amazing and often immediate effect. Years and years of unforgiveness and hardened attitudes can break up and dissolve in a matter of minutes! And why is this level of consciousness so powerful? Because It operates only in love; It knows only love, sees only love.

This Christ love, sincerely radiated, eventually proves irresistible. Barriers come down and defenses fall in the face of this Giving consciousness. No one is exempt because the Christ-consciousness is all inclusive!!!

It is why we are called to put aside our old hurts and attitudes—to no longer choose to let these kinds of emotions dictate the nature of our relationships. We must take on new habits of thought. Often, learning new practices of interaction and developing new understandings help us bridge the gap between our "inherited" ways of interacting and our desire to give from our Christ Consciousness. A cautionary note, however: Even though we are going to be exploring a set of skills to help us in creating more supportive relationships, we must remember that the origination point for learning these skills must be the desire to operate from our "giving" consciousness—not to "fix" others!!!

Practice: Conscious Communication

People are not disturbed by things, but by the view they take of them.
Epictetus

Conscious Communication is so important a skill that everyone of us should insist that it be taught in school from the time one is in the first grade. I have read over and over again that it is the lack of good communication skills that cause more people to quit, leave or get fired from jobs than anything else. So, this is a skill we can use everywhere—within our intimate relationships, with our family and friends and also on the job.

So what makes conscious communication different from ordinary communication? What makes it different is the mindset with which we approach the communication. A couple of the authors I have read refer to this act of communication as the art of being able to genuinely say to the other: "Tell me More". It is the art of being able to listen from a place of total compassion. In this place, you, the listener, are not holding your breath waiting to say your piece. You are not on the defensive but are coming from a place of genuinely wanting to hear and understand the hurt and pain of the other. It does not mean you must agree with it, only that you understand and empathize with the other's perception of the situation. The best way I know to describe the mind set with which the listener must come to the communication is that of seeing each other as on the same team. Because we are both on the same team, we can and will work this out to our mutual benefit.

There are a number of resources one can use to learn more about conscious communication, but the one I am most familiar with and do my best to practice in my relationships with others is based on the work of Marshall Rosenberg. He has written a number of books on the subject; my ideas are drawn from two of his books: *Practical Spirituality* [1] and *Non-Violent*

Communication. [2]. Many of my specific examples are drawn from the work of a friend and colleague, Linda Dunn, who teaches courses in Mediation and Conflict Resolution. [3]

Rosenberg's book *Non-Violent Communication* came out of his attempt to understand the concept of love and how to manifest it. He came to the conclusion that it is not just something we feel, but it is something we manifest. And what is this manifestation? It's to give of ourselves through an honest expression of what is alive in us in this moment.

Every culture has an expression such as*: How are you?* We say it as a ritual, but it's really an important question because if we're to live in peace and harmony, if we're to enjoy contributing to one another's well-being, we need to know what's alive in one another. To give a gift of oneself is a manifestation of love. It's a gift when we reveal ourselves unabashedly, at any given moment, for no other purpose than to reveal what's alive in us. Not to blame, criticize or punish. Just: "Here I am, and here is what I would like." This is my vulnerability in this moment. To me this is a way of manifesting love. The other way we give of ourselves is in how we receive another's message. We want to receive it empathically, connecting with what's important, making no judgement. Our goal is simply to hear what's alive in them and what they would like.

Rosenberg says of his work: "Consensus building is a spiritual practice. Why? Because consensus building is a practice, a way of life that allows us to see and hear the other in ways we may not have ever done before. I hope eventually we will come to see that it's more than a communication process and realize that it's really an attempt to manifest our spirituality." [4]

His hope is that his process helps people make sure the spirituality that's guiding us is one of our own choosing and not the "inherited purpose" we have internalized from our culture. He believes as I do that the language of our culture prevents us from knowing our Divine Energy more intimately. He goes on to say: "We live in a destructive mythology that requires a certain language. It requires a language that dehumanizes people, turns them into objects. So, we have learned to think in moralistic judgments of one another. We have words in our consciousness like right, wrong, good, bad, selfish, unselfish, terrorists, freedom fighters." [5]

As we now turn to the specifics of his communication process, we learn more about how to avoid moralistic judgments and instead state what is "alive" for us in the moment. In any communication process, there are actually two parts. If I am going to share what is "alive" in me, then there must be someone on the other end who's receiving my message. For the moment, let's think of one as the giver of the message and the other as the receiver of the message. No matter which role you are playing, there are still four parts to the communication process. They are: observations, feelings, needs and requests.

Let's begin looking at this 4-step process through the eyes of the message "giver". As the message "giver", you start with an observation:

- **OBSERVATIONS**—When you make an observation, you are describing what is happening in the moment. It may or may not be creating a problem for you, but usually it is, which is why you want to bring the situation to the other person's attention in the first place!

  The "key" is to simply describe. **Refrain from interpreting** what you are seeing or hearing. That comes later. You may use words like "When I see you talking to…or "When I hear you say… or "When you arrive ten minutes after our agreed upon time, …

  Below are some examples. Let's see if you can distinguish between describing words and judging words. HINT: Judging words can be either positive or negative! Simply draw a circle around each number that represents a describing sentence.

  1. "You lied to me about how you were doing in school."
  2. "My husband hardly ever expresses affection."
  3. "You wore my necklace without first getting my permission."
  4. "Jake told me I didn't look good in green."
  5. "Jane was first in line every day this week".

6. "Robert was angry with me yesterday for no reason."

Now, let's check out how well you did. If you circled number 1, then you and I don't see eye to eye. In the first sentence above, the word <u>lied</u> is a "judging" word. If, instead, I had said something like: "When I asked about your school grades, you told me you had passed all of your courses, but, today, I received a phone call from your teacher who shared with me that you were failing two classes."

If you circled number 2, you and I don't see eye to eye. In this sentence, the words "expresses affection" is a judgment. We have no idea what this person really wants when she makes this statement. It would be more accurate for her to say: "My husband hasn't hugged me in two weeks."

If you circled number 3, you and I are in one accord—that's assuming the two people already had an agreement that permission was a pre-requisite to wearing the jewelry. Otherwise, a clarification sentence might be in order first such as: "It is my understanding we had an agreement you would not wear my jewelry without first getting my permission."

If you circled 4, you and I are in one accord so long as the speaker is simply stating what the other person said. It is important to note that Jake was making an evaluation. If Jake had said "I don't think the color green looks good on you. That would have been a more accurate statement from Jake because he would be owning his opinion. Instead he made a statement which he "generalized" to imply that everyone would be in agreement with his statement.

If you circled 5, you and I are in one accord. This sentence states a simple observation without any value judgements attached to it.

If you circled 6, you and I do not see eye to eye. Firstly, the expression "for no reason" is an evaluation rather than a description of the behavior. And secondly, when you say that Robert is "angry", you could be making a false assumption about what's actually "alive" in Robert. He could be feeling hurt, sad or something else—not necessarily anger. Another option that perhaps describes Robert's behavior more accurately would be to say that "Robert raised his voice when he spoke to me."

- **FEELINGS**—In the second step, it's important to describe our feelings about the observation we have just made. Sometimes, we confuse words that express our feelings with our thoughts about a situation. For example, we might use words like attacked, betrayed, discounted to describe our feelings. These are actually not descriptions of feelings, but rather evaluation words. Descriptions of feelings include words such as: hurt, angry, scared, disappointed, bewildered, confused, embarrassed, thwarted, etc.

Comfortable feelings indicate our needs are being met. Uncomfortable feelings indicate our needs are not being met.

The English language allows us to use the word "feel" without actually expressing a feeling. It is, therefore, critical in learning to express our feelings to make certain distinctions. They are:

1. **Distinguish between thought and feelings**
   Feelings are not clearly expressed when the word **feel** is followed by:
   Words such as ***that, like, as if***:
   "**I feel that** you should know better."
   "**I feel like** I'm a failure."
   "**I feel as if** I am living with a wall."
   Pronouns ***I, you, he, she it, they***:
   "**I feel I** am constantly on call."
   "**I feel it** is useless."
   "**I feel she** is trying to undermine me."
   Names or nouns ***referring to people***:
   "**I feel Amy** has been very irresponsible."
   "**I feel my colleague** is being manipulative.

2. **Distinguish between what we feel and who we think we are.**

There are words in English we use after the word **feel**, which are actually thoughts or judgments we make about ourselves. For example:

"I feel inadequate as a mother." In this statement I am judging my abilities as a mother. (The following three sentences could more accurately describe how I am feeling.):

"I feel so frustrated as a mother."

"I feel disappointed in myself as a mother."

"I feel overwhelmed by the demands of motherhood."

3. **Distinguish between what we feel and how we think others react or behave toward us.**

In English, some words we use after the word **feel** are actually thoughts or judgments we have about how others are behaving toward us. For example:

"I feel misunderstood." (Here the word "misunderstood" indicates my judgment of the other person's understanding rather than an actual feeling such as **"hopeless** or **"annoyed".)

"I feel disrespected." (This is a judgment of how I see others treating me, rather than a clear statement of how I am feeling. I could feel

astonished, annoyed, disgusted, humiliated, frustrated or hurt.)

When we are expressing a feeling, we do not need to use the word "feel", we can simply say, **"I'm irritated, worried, excited, etc."**

Below are some examples of sentences that may or may not actually be expressing a feeling. Let's see if you can distinguish between words that express a feeling and words that express a thought or an evaluation. Simply draw a circle around each number that represents an expression of a feeling.

We are going to build on the sentences we began with in the Observation activity.

1. ("When I asked about your school grades, you told me you had passed all of your courses. But, today, I received a phone call from your teacher who shared with me that you were failing two classes.) **I feel you can't be trusted**."
2. **"I feel frustrated** (when my husband doesn't hug me every day.")
3. **"I'm upset** (you wore my necklace without first getting permission.")
4. (When Jake told me I didn't look good in green), **I felt like a loser**."
5. **"I get upset** (when I am already in line and Jane gets in line ahead of me.")
6. **"I was angry** (with Robert for raising his voice at me yesterday.")

If you circled 1, you and I do not see eye to eye. In this sentence you are making a judgment about the other person rather than expressing a feeling. A feeling might be something like "I am feeling frustrated because…or I get anxious because…or I was disappointed because… Remember: When the words "I feel" are followed by I, you, he, she, they, it's usually not expressing a feeling.

If you circled 2, you and I are in one accord that a feeling was verbally expressed. You will notice that in this sentence the feeling is expressed first followed by the observation.

If you circled 3, you and I are in one accord that a feeling was expressed. You will notice that in this sentence the feeling is also expressed first followed by the observation.

If you circled 4, you and I do not see eye to eye. The expression, "I felt like a loser" does not express a feeling, but rather a self-evaluation. Words one might use to express a feeling in this sentence might be disappointed, indignant, embarrassed.

If you circled 5, you and I are in one accord that a feeling was verbally expressed.

CHARLOTTE F. LEHECKA, PHD

If you circled 6, you and I are in one accord that a feeling was verbally expressed.

We have now looked at two parts of our four-part communication model. We have learned to distinguish between an observation and an evaluation and to determine if we are expressing a feeling or making an evaluation. You may have noticed that there is no set way for these two parts to come in a sentence. Sometimes the observation comes first followed by an expression of feeling and other times, the feeling comes first followed by the observation. You'll notice in the sentences above that I've frequently added the word "because". That's because BECAUSE leads us into the third part of the communication process—needs!

- **NEEDS**—This third step in the communication process addresses our values, desires, expectations or thoughts that are creating the feelings. This is the step in the process where we accept responsibility for what we do to generate our own feelings. What others do may be the stimulus for our feelings, but it is not the cause. Here, we learn that our feelings result from our particular needs and expectations in the moment.

  When we accept responsibility for our feelings, by acknowledging our own needs, desires, expectations, values or thoughts, it brings the responsibility for our communication back to us. We must let go of the notion that the other person, the situation, i.e.— anything *out there* is responsible for our feelings. We, and only we, are responsible. By taking full responsibility for our feelings, our words and our actions, we are in a position to "pay attention" to what <u>need</u> in us is not being fulfilled rather than focusing outward and blaming others or the situation for what's going on inside of us.

  Below are a couple of examples to help you make the distinction between owning the interaction yourself and blaming others for the feelings you are experiencing.

Example 1:
  A. You disappointed me by not coming over last night."
  B. "I was disappointed when you didn't come over because I wanted to talk over some things that were bothering me.

Notice how Speaker A uses the pronoun 'you" thereby attributing responsibility for the disappointment solely to the action of the other person. In B, the speaker uses the pronoun "I" twice to demonstrate they are taking responsibility for their feelings. With the first "I" statement, they are expressing a feeling of disappointment. With the second "I" statement, the speaker traces their feelings to a desire that is not being fulfilled. He had a need "to talk over some things…".

Example 2:
  A. "Their cancelling the contract really irritated me!"
  B. "When they cancelled the contract, I felt really irritated because I was thinking to myself that it was an awfully irresponsible thing to do."

Speaker A attributes her irritation solely to the behavior of the other party. Speaker B accepts her responsibility for her feelings by acknowledging the thought behind it. Thus far we have an example of her feelings and the thought behind it, but we still don't know what her actual need is in this situation. "Why" is she so annoyed. To get at her annoyance, we have to ask the question: "What need, desire, etc. is not being fulfilled by the loss of this contract?" She could, for example, have been "excited" instead of "annoyed". She could have said: "When they cancelled the contract, I was actually excited because I was thinking to myself that I had more work than I could effectively manage at this point in time."

Hopefully, it's becoming clearer and clearer how important it is to understand what's triggering our feelings. And recognize them as our feelings, not something the other person did or said. In the

CHARLOTTE F. LEHECKA, PHD

above example, her irritation was caused by a need/desire she had to re-hire the workers she had laid off the year before.

Judgments, criticisms, diagnoses and interpretations of others are alienated expressions of our needs. "You didn't come to my presentation; you must not value our friendship very much." In this sentence, I have managed to diagnose and interpret the motivation of the other rather than stating my unmet need. My unmet need in this instance is to feel positive, supportive energy radiating from my friends while I'm presenting. However, when I express my need indirectly through the use of evaluations, interpretations and images, if you are like me, I hear your statement as criticism and immediately become defensive.

If we are wishing for a compassionate response from others, it is self-defeating to express our needs by interpreting or diagnosing their behavior. Instead, the more directly we can connect our feelings to our own needs, the easier it is for others to respond compassionately to our needs.

No matter from what country you come, what your religious background is, or what your age is, needs are basically the same. An example of some of the universal needs we all have are: autonomy, celebration, integrity, interdependence, physical nurturance, play and spiritual communion.

In a world where we are often judged harshly for revealing our needs, doing so can be very frightening, especially for women who are socialized to ignore their own needs while caring for others.

In our next exercise, we want to identify the needs which are at the root of the feelings. We will continue using the sentences we began with in steps 1 and 2 of the compassionate communication process. Please draw a circle around the number in front of any statement where the speaker is acknowledging responsibility for his or her needs. Remember: Universal Needs center around some basic issues like trust, security, respect, fear, etc.

1. "When I asked about your school grades, you told me you had passed all of your courses. But, today, I received a phone call from your teacher who shared with me that you were failing two classes. I am disappointed **because you never do what you say you're going to do.**
2. "I feel frustrated when my husband doesn't hug me every day **because physical touch is how I experience love.**"
3. "I'm upset you wore my necklace without first getting permission **as it sends a message to me that you can't be trusted.**"
4. "When Jake told me I didn't look good in green, I felt embarrassed. **Little things people say sometimes hurt me.**"
5. "I was upset because Jane kept getting in line ahead of me **because I value fairness and when she gets in line ahead of me without asking me if it's okay, I don't like it.**"
6. "I was angry with Robert for raising his voice at me yesterday." **He should be more considerate of others' feelings.**

If you drew a circle around number 1, you and I do not see eye to eye. The expression "because you never do what you say you are going to do" implies that the other person's behavior is solely responsible for the speaker's feelings. It doesn't reveal the speaker's needs or thoughts that are contributing to his or her feelings. The person might have said, "I get disappointed because I'm thinking this person can't be trusted and honesty is an important value to me."

If you drew a circle around number 2, you and I are in one accord that the speaker is acknowledging responsibility for her feelings.

If you drew a circle around number 3, you and I do not see eye to eye. To express the needs and thoughts underlying her feelings, the speaker might have said, "I'm upset you wore my necklace without first getting permission because I want to be able to rely on your words."

If you drew a circle around number 4, you and I do not see eye to eye. "Little things people say sometimes hurt me" is not acknowledging the need I have in this situation. The speaker might have said: "I feel embarrassed because I want others to be in agreement with me about my choices".

If you drew a circle around number 5, you and I are in one accord that the speaker is acknowledging responsibility for his/her needs based on their values.

If you drew a circle around number 6, you and I do not see eye to eye. The speaker's statement makes a judgement about the other person's behavior, it does not acknowledge the speaker's possible need for safety, consideration or respect. The following response would more accurately capture the person's needs: "I get on the defensive immediately when I perceive another person criticizing me and I would like to be able to hear what the other person is needing from me."

We have now covered three of the four parts of an effective communication strategy. Now we are going to explore the last part.

- **REQUESTS**—The fourth and final part of this model addresses the question: If we are experiencing unmet needs, what would we like to request of the other? Rosenberg says that when we make a request of the other, we are asking for something we believe will enrich our lives in some way. The question becomes: How do we express our requests in such a way that the other is open and willing to respond to our needs.

  One of the first points I want to emphasize is that when we are making a request, we request what it is we want, not what we don't want. Here's an example of what I mean: In this scenario, the wife wanted her husband to spend more time at home with her and the kids, but what she said was: "I'd appreciate it if you spent less time at work." So, what did the husband do? He organized a basketball game once a week with his friends. And, in doing so, he's thinking he has responded positively to his wife's request!!! What she failed to do was make **a positive statement** about what she really wanted.

In addition to using positive language, we also want to avoid vague language and, instead, word our requests in the form of clear, specific, concrete actions another can take. Let's take the example above. In this scenario, the wife could ask him to spend at least one evening a week at home with her and the children.

Sometimes, when we make a request, we may wonder if the person accurately heard our request. In those instances, it's always good to ask for a reflection, i.e., "Would you do me a favor and share with me what you just heard me say?" If they give a positive, accurate response, we express our appreciation. But sometimes what is said and what is heard are two very different things. In those instances, it's important to—not make the other wrong—but take responsibility for the communication and try again.

Sometimes, however, because of people's past baggage either with you or others in their lives, they may react to any request as a demand and immediately go on the defensive. They may submit but resent or they may rebel. A dear friend of mine, Linda Dunn, who teaches conscious communication skills actually prefers to treat the request part of the model in a more generic way. She teaches her participants to preface any request with the statement: "Would you be willing to consider…? Saying this has the advantage of softening your request so that the other is more able to hear it as a request.

And lastly, you need to also check in with yourself: Are you simply making a request or is it really a demand? How you know the answer to that question is how you respond to their answer. If they respond positively, no problem; but if they say "no" and you get upset, guess what? You've just made a demand! For it to be a true request, you must be okay with a "no". Let me give you an example. I've often heard parents request of their children: "Please go brush your teeth." The child refuses and the conversation escalates. If not brushing the teeth is not an option, then a situation like this requires the parent to give options: "It's time to brush your teeth, do you want to do it or do you want me to do it for you?" At least, in this scenario, the child has some freedom to still make choices.

To summarize: our objective in conscious communication is not to change people and their behavior in order to get our way. It is to establish relationships based on honesty and empathy which will eventually meet everyone's needs.

In our next exercise, we want to identify the requests and determine if they are truly a request or a demand in disguise. We will continue using the sentences we began with in steps 1,2 and 3 of the compassionate communication process. Please draw a circle around the number in front of any statement where the speaker is clearly requesting that a specific action be taken.

1. "When I asked about your school grades, you told me you had passed all of your courses. But, today, I received a phone call from your teacher who shared with me that you were failing two classes. I am disappointed because I'm thinking this person can't be trusted and honesty is an important value to me." **I want you to stop lying to me.**
2. "I feel frustrated when my husband doesn't hug me every day because physical touch is how I experience love." **Would you be willing to hug me at least once a day?**
3. "I'm upset you wore my necklace without first getting permission because I want to be able to rely on your words. **I'd like you to show respect for my belongings.**
4. "When Jake told me I didn't look good in green, I felt embarrassed because I want others to be in agreement with me about my choices." **I'd like you to let me be me.**
5. "I was upset because you (Jane) got in line ahead of me. I value fairness and when you get in line ahead of me without asking me if it's okay, I don't like it." **Would you help me understand what need of yours is being met by getting in line ahead of me?**

6. "I was angry with (you) Robert for raising your voice at me yesterday. I get on the defensive immediately when I perceive another person criticizing me and I would like to be able to hear what the other person is needing from me." **Would you be willing to share with me what you heard me saying?**

If you drew a circle around number 1, you and I do not see eye to eye. The expression "I want you to stop lying to me" does not really express what the speaker wants but rather what he or she doesn't want. The speaker might have said: "I'm wondering if you could share with me how I need to express myself so that you feel safe in telling me what's really going on with you."

If you drew a circle around number 2, you and I are in one accord that the speaker has made her request clearly and specifically and has asked for concrete actions of the other.

If you drew a circle around number 3, you and I do not see eye to eye. The statement: "I'd like you to show respect for my belongings" does not address the speaker's need to be able to count on the person to keep their word. One might have said: "Would you be willing to check with me before using my jewelry in the future?"

If you drew a circle around number 4, you and I do not see eye to eye. The statement: "I'd like you to let me be me" does not clearly express a specific action to be taken. The speaker might have said: "I appreciate your willingness to let me express my feelings. It helps me see how unrealistic they are and I want to thank you in advance for giving me your honest opinion as I just realized I value honesty over my need to always have you agree with me".

If you drew a circle around number 5, you and I are in one accord that the speaker is making a legitimate request of the other by asking for clarity concerning the other's need to get in front of her in a non-threatening way.

If you drew a circle around number 6, you and I are in one accord. The speaker is requesting the listener to reiterate what they heard the speaker say.

To summarize this section on conscious communication, we have looked at the importance of bringing compassion to our interactions with one another and learned some tools that will make our future communication with others more life-giving. It's important to remember that we are on both the giving and receiving end of every communication with another.

Not only does this communication model give us an opportunity to ask for those things which will make our lives more joyful, but it also gives us the opportunity to bring joy to another by truly listening when the other expresses an unmet need to us. I encourage you to remind yourself frequently when another comes to you with a request: "We are both on the same team!" That reminder will help you be free of judgment and able to put yourself in a space to listen from the heart.

FIVE

POUR ME OUT A BLESSING

Prose

Things may happen around you,
and things may happen to you,
but the only things that really count
are the things that happen in you.

Eric Butterworth

Several years ago when I penned this story, I was unemployed, so you might be asking yourself—how, under those circumstances, could she possibly have a prosperity story to share with us? And yet, I stand before you today making the claim that I never felt so wealthy as I did during that time of my life.

Perhaps there are some of you who have already learned how to be financially prosperous and hopefully you too will enjoy my story, but this story is really for those of you who may not be feeling so prosperous, who may even be feeling overwhelmed by your circumstances at the moment. This is for the ones who are not sure how you are going to pay this week's bills.

Now let me lay the groundwork for you. A couple of years before I was laid off, I began to experience what I like to call "divine discontent". I have always loved my work, but it was just not fulfilling me like it had in the past. Also, I was tired of the pressure of the life of an entrepreneur, so I made the decision to take a job with a "secure" income teaching German at the local high school. It was a part time job, and, of course, along with a part time job comes part time pay.

At first, I thought I'd be able to work that job and something else on the weekends to make ends meet, but I soon learned that although the German was part time in pay, it was not part time when it came to preparing for and delivering these classes. So, I found myself quickly reduced to an income that was only a third of what I had been earning. But I rationalized—it is okay to go from an income of $65,000 a year to about $24,000 because—by adding a class to the German program each year my income would increase. By year 2, I would be able to pay my bills and in three years, I would actually be making an income that would give me the financial freedom I was seeking without the hassle of entrepreneurship. So, with my plan in hand, I poured my heart into my German classes and began taking out substantial sums from my savings to subsidize myself.

Just before the end of my first year of teaching German, I was called into the principal's office and told that due to the current economic situation, the new German program was being cut. So much for my plan!!! It is the only time in my life I had ever been laid off.

I began immediately applying for other jobs, but nothing happened. Months drug on—six to be exact—before I had any kind of employment, but I will tell you more about that later. There was a job I was interested in which was scheduled to begin in September 2009. Each month, I would be told—it's going to start up the next month, and then the next month. And mind you all of this time I was continuing to make hefty withdrawals from my savings. I was really scared. Here I was using up my savings at a fast clip with no income prospects. I was definitely into "poverty consciousness".

Then comes January 2010. Our minister, Rev. Catherine, began a sermon series on Abundance. This is where the story starts to get really interesting. Rev. Catherine based her series on Edwina Gaines' book, *The Four Spiritual Laws of Prosperity*. In her book, Edwina talks about being at wits end with her finances—sitting on the floor crying and, in despair, shouting out: "Now, see here God! I believe it when Jesus said, 'I have come that you might have life, and live it abundantly.' So, I don't think he lied to us, but I am obviously not living abundantly. Show me how?"

At this time, she had no prayer life, was not involved with any church, but she still had a healthy respect for the Bible, so she opened it up and it fell open to the following scripture: *Bring all of the tithes into the storehouse—If you do, says the Lord Almighty, I will open the windows of heaven for you. I will pour out such a blessing that you won't have enough room to take it in! Try it! Let me prove it to you! (Malachi 3:10)* But Edwina's thinking was: "I can't afford to tithe. I can't even afford to properly care for my daughter. How could I give away 10 percent of my money?" She thought to herself: "There is no way I could be so irresponsible. The whole idea of me giving away the little money I have is outrageous."

So, as I'm reading this, I'm thinking: "It would be really, really great to have the windows of heaven open up for me. It seems that all of my life, even though I have experienced abundance in many, many areas, when it comes to financial prosperity, I seem to—only—just scrape by. And I am really tired of always feeling afraid that I will not have the money to take care of myself—especially as I grow older.

I wasn't too sure that tithing was the answer as I'd been tithing 10% of my income for some time—even during this time of unemployment when I had just kept tithing the same 10% I had been tithing before being laid off. On the one hand, I would have to admit that—despite being laid off and despite tithing, my bills were somehow all getting paid and yet I was aware that I still had a lot of fear and anxiety around my finances—this feeling of poverty consciousness.

I didn't want to just have enough money to get by, I wanted to really feel abundant. So, what should I do? Then, further on in the book, I read where someone decided to tithe at the level of the income they wanted, not what they currently had. So, I said to myself—"Okay, that's what I'm going to do. I'm going to stretch beyond my comfort zone. I want to see what happens if I begin tithing at an even higher rate."

To get into the spirit of abundance, one of the things Edwina Gaines suggests is tithing on every source of money. This got to be a wonderful, joy-filled activity. If I found a dime on the ground, I would make sure I tithed a penny of it. I kept a record of all the monies that came in and then thought about where I wanted to tithe. I also began immediately tithing by check an additional $10 a week to my spiritual community over and above the monthly automatic withdrawal. I did that because of my promise to myself to tithe at the amount I wanted to receive and because it felt really good to write a check each week and bless it and put it in the offering plate.

From this point on, things started to happen. First, one of my brothers sent me a gift of $2000. After tithing on that money, I took the rest and set up a savings account because I had begun to see that one of the things that fueled my "poverty consciousness" was the anxiety I experienced each month around paying my monthly bills. Knowing that I had that money as back-up took the pressure off. I felt rich. I set up all of my accounts on automatic withdrawal, so I didn't even have to think about bills. They were just automatically paid each month. And that is still true today!

Next thing that happened, you remember the job I kept getting told—next month, next month, well guess when it finally materialized? You guessed it—January. When I first began, it was only one quarter hours, but 3 weeks into teaching this course, the other instructor was unable to continue and I suddenly had a half- time teaching job, the income from which allowed me to quit taking money from my savings.

I was so relieved as it had been really scary watching my life savings—my retirement money—dwindling at such a fast clip. But actually, it wasn't dwindling. That was my poverty consciousness talking. In point of fact, what I actually became aware of was that, although I was taking out $1500 each month, by the next month, when I was to take out money again, it was back to the same level it had been the month before. What an incredible phenomenon! Only I wasn't ready to appreciate this fact. I wasn't ready to experience it as a blessing. I was still too much into my "poverty consciousness". Rather than seeing it for the blessing it was, I was only able to feel regret that I was depleting my life savings.

What was I going to live on when I retired? Finally, I began to notice what I was saying to myself and feel how thinking those thoughts of regret and fear were making me feel. I began to see how deeply ingrained my "poverty consciousness" truly was. So with that insight, I began to think: "How can I reframe this experience, so that I no longer see it as a "negative" but as a "plus"? because by this time, I had come to truly appreciate that changing my consciousness is the "key" to moving out of poverty into abundance. So, I asked myself "why" was I feeling "bad" about taking money out of my savings account each month. I was no longer touching the original investment. Each month I was simply using the interest that accrued. Couldn't I just see this as a present from God each month and be totally grateful? I decided I could do that and now I am ecstatic each month that I have this—what feels to me like a money tree—in my back yard that I may draw upon to support me.

So—let's move ahead to 2011. The teaching job only lasted for four months and I was back looking for work again, but between unemployment insurance and my money tree, my regular and ordinary bills were continuing to get paid. However, I still had three out-of-the ordinary expenses for which I needed money—my porch roof had a leak and needed to be fixed. I did not want to drive my car another summer without air conditioning and I had a tooth that my dentist said needed a new crown.

I began to become aware that I hadn't *expanded my consciousness* to include those repairs. I was still harboring a "just getting by" mentality. While I was grateful that my regular bills were being paid, I still hadn't felt I could ask the universe for more. When I became aware of this, I asked myself—why haven't you told the universe that you also want these things taken care of? And so I determined that if God could provide for all of the other things, It could also take care of these additional items. I just needed to do as the scriptures instructed and ask.

I needed $800 for the AC repair. I put it out to the universe, made the appointment to get the car repaired and within the week—before the repair job was scheduled—my other brother and his wife sent me a check for $300 and my daughter sent me a check for $200 for Mother's Day. All of a sudden with the money I had saved, I had the needed money for the AC.

I am going into such detail because I want you to see—that it is not about us talking God into doing anything so much as it is about us gradually <u>expanding our consciousness</u> to accept the abundance that is always there for us. We just have to claim it.

I want to reiterate that I believe these changes were coming about—not necessarily because I began tithing 22% instead of 10%—but because <u>tithing increases our faith</u> in the abundance of the universe. What I have learned is that it is critical to just do it. And do it first, give your tithe money before you pay another bill. Commit to it. It's your fear mentality that you want to overcome.

This is how you overcome the fear, by committing to something and then just watching what happens. Watch how you feel when you see that—even though you gave money you did not think you had to give away—that when you did it, everything seemed to work out somehow. Pay attention to how it feels to be a giver. The joy you experience from giving. Then, notice how you feel when you withhold out of fear. Which feeling had you rather experience?

There's a famous quote I want to share with you that I believe captures this experience beautifully. The quote is from W. H. Murray and it goes like this:

> But when I said that nothing had been done, I erred in one important matter. We had definitely committed ourselves and were halfway out of our ruts. We had put down our passage money—booked a sailing to Bombay. This may sound too simple but is great in consequence. Until one is committed, there is hesitancy, the chance to draw back, always ineffectiveness. Concerning all acts of initiative (and creation), there is one elementary truth the ignorance of which kills countless ideas and splendid plans: that the moment one definitely commits oneself, then providence moves too. A whole stream of events issues from the decision, raising in one's favor all manner of unforeseen incidents, meetings and material assistance, which no man could have dreamt would have come his way. [1]

But let me continue with my story.

So, I hope you can see from my story that there's a pattern. And the pattern is what? Our needs are provided for—often even before we ask. Our job is to be willing to go where we are guided—to open up to the flow. Contrary to what we have been programmed to believe, this Universe—if we will allow it—WILL SUPPORT US—ABUNDANTLY.

I still have not rid myself of all of my poverty consciousness, but as I learn to have faith that the Universe will and is taking care of me, it gets less and less every day.

Principle

We will now look at several key principles operating within this story. They are: 1) the Law of Circulation, 2) the Law of Prosperity/ Expanding our Consciousness, and 3) the Law of Gratitude and the practices which support each of these principles.

The Law of Circulation

The Law of Circulation states that—whatever we want more of in our lives—begin by giving it away. If we want more love, then give love away. If we want better financial health, then give financially. I know it's scary—it feels like when we have so little we need to hold it tight, but the lesson I have learned is that the more I am able to let go of "fear" and "lack", the more abundant my life has become. So, let's look at this Law of Circulation in more detail.

> *You are prosperous to the degree that you are experiencing peace, health, and plenty in your world.—Catherine Ponder*

Financial prosperity is actually a subset of a broader topic which I like to refer to as abundance. For when we have abundance in our lives, it is referring to more than financial prosperity, it is also referring to physical health, love, rewarding service or vocation, etc. And creating abundance in our lives comes about when we practice the law of circulation. Often when we think on these topics, we think of getting –getting money, love, health, the perfect work—but actually the way it works is just the opposite.

To get these things in our lives is to first give these things. And give them unconditionally so that Source Energy flows through us unimpeded. If you want more love, give love. If you want better financial health, give your money on a consistent basis to those places that serve you spiritually. You might ask: Why is this true? It's true because when we give, we honor the Source from which all gifts come. When we give we show our faith and trust in God as our Source. When we give we are saying to Source, we trust you to provide for us in every way. And even more, we are recognizing that since Source Energy is everywhere present that means it is present in us as us too. We simply need reminders of this Truth.

In the Prose section, I mentioned the scripture: *Bring all of the tithes into the storehouse—If you do, says the Lord Almighty, I will open the windows of heaven for you. I will pour out such a blessing that you won't have enough room to take it in! Try it! Let me prove it to you!* (Malachi 3:10) It was this very scripture that got my attention, but it is not the only scripture. There are others. At this moment in my life, I have been reminding myself as I go through my day of the first line of the 23rd Psalm which says: *God is my shepherd, I shall not want.* (Psalm 23:1) I shall not want. I shall not want. I shall not want for any good thing. So if I am to trust that God is my Source and that God is everywhere present and that God is willing to provide for our every need, that must mean that God is the source of my health, my love, my finances, my everything!!!

If God is the source of everything, why is it then important that I need to give too? Because God or Source or whatever name you wish to call It runs this universe using certain immutable laws. One of those laws is called the Law of Circulation. This law operates whether I choose to cooperate with it or not. However when I cooperate with this law from a place of unconditional love and gratitude, I stay in the divine flow of life and Life can do nothing else but bless me. That is Life's promise to me.

Practice: Financial tithing.

While prosperity or abundance is a topic which is really bigger than financial health, in this practice we turn our focus specifically to financial abundance. So, let's look at how we can tithe our way to financial abundance.

We know from our study of the Bible that the Jewish people were required to tithe one-tenth of their income. We saw from my story what can happen when we make a habit of joyfully giving one tenth of our financial wealth to the place that nourishes us spiritually. Do you think that God needs our money? Well, yes and no. If we understand that God expresses through us and that God's desire is for each of us to have an abundant life, then if we refuse to participate in the Law of Circulation, we are basically cutting off God's ability to give through us. On the other hand, when we say "yes" to God's willingness to give us our hearts desires and accept the good that the Universe continually wants to bless us with, then the overall consciousness of the universe is expanded.

If you go back to this scripture that I got so excited about, it says: …test me. God is saying you don't have to take my word for it, test me, test me. So, I invite you to test this theory as I did. Test it—commit to tithing for six months and see what happens.

So what is the real point of tithing? I have asked myself why ten percent? Why not five percent? Or fifteen or twenty percent? I believe that we've been asked to give ten percent because it's enough to stretch us, to cause us to expand our faith, our trust in God's promise that we are truly living in a giving, abundant universe.

Ten percent, I believe, is also just a starting point. We can also tithe more and the more we tithe, the more our faith in God's promise increases. Consequently, our financial blessings also increase for as the old saying goes, WE CANNOT OUTGIVE GOD!

The real point of tithing is to take action that assists us in sustaining a "giving" consciousness. And as our consciousness expands, our faith expands, and we are able to give more and more. When we cultivate a giving consciousness, we feel rich. When we feel rich, we are rich—and we are free from fear. Butterworth tells us, "Tithing is not an end but a helpful means towards the end of totally living in a giving consciousness." [2]

Tithing is the teaching tool used to graduate us into a giving consciousness. If everyone were in a totally giving consciousness, there would be no need for tithing. And we would be living in a very different world!

However, since that is not yet the case, we are called to take baby steps toward that goal. And that first baby step is tithing. So, let's take a deeper dive into tithing! Here are some critical steps, synthesized from Edwene Gaines' book, *The Four Spiritual Laws of Prosperity*, to remember:

1. **Consistency**—If we want the Universe to give to us on a consistent basis then we must give on a consistent basis.

2. **Tithe First**—We are asked to tithe first—BEFORE we pay our bills or do anything else with our money. When I first began tithing in earnest that was a daunting "fear" I had to overcome. What really helped me was not to think too much about it, but to just do it and see what happened.

3. **Tithe where you are spiritually fed**—It's important to tithe toward resource and not need. Our concern is to acknowledge God as our source by giving 10 percent to those who feed us spiritual food. This does not solely mean the spiritual community in which we participate. It can be anyone or place that nourishes us spiritually. For example, I give to several organizations who focus on the environment because being out in nature feeds my soul. I have also tithed to a friend or a colleague who lifted me up by their nurturing presence. When we tithe to those people or places who have nourished our spiritual life, we are honoring the Immanence of God in and around us. If you have questions about where to tithe, ask in prayer: Where have I received spiritual food? Then follow the guidance you receive.

4. **Tithe on ALL sources of income**—salary, bonuses, interest earned, monetary gifts, dividends, proceeds from the sale of a house, and money we win, inherit, or find on the street. Everything! No matter through what channel it came, it's origin is God.

5. **Tithe on your gross income**—When you tithe on your gross income, you are sending a message to your sub-conscious that you are serious about your commitment to prosperity. And God always honors a cheerful giver. If you are nitpicking about gross or net, what message are you sending? Is it "How little can I get by with and still be okay?" and is that not a fearful, limiting stance? Rather than ask that question it's better to develop faith that God is your Source and Source wants to provide for you abundantly. (3)

In addition to tithing, another element evidenced in my story is the idea of "expanding our consciousness" to receive. We will look at this principle next.

Law of Prosperity/ Expanding our Consciousness

I open the gates of my consciousness to receive
the abundant blessings God has in store for me.
I let go of limitation and embrace my amazing new life.

Sometimes I don't even know that I'm holding a limiting belief around something, but then I begin to look at my circumstances and recognize that I must be holding some kind of limiting belief around this situation because, otherwise, life would be showing up differently. In this situation, I've recognized it's not the Universe holding something back from me because the Universe is always a giver to life. Then—if not the universe— it must be that I am holding some limiting belief. In the past, I might have beat up on myself or spent hours trying to figure out what I'd done "wrong". Nowadays, I simply bless the situation and keep blessing it and keep blessing it while knowing that all will be revealed in divine timing and divine order. Sometimes, we learn that there are some pre-requisite steps we need to take before we can be ready for whatever it is we are asking for, or that there are others who have to be ready too for the demonstration to take place.

Mary Morrisey, [4] a teacher in the realm of prosperity consciousness, shared the following story about her son in one of her seminars. Her son was selling real estate and wanted to join the million dollar a year sales group. He was so close, but it seemed that one thing after another kept happening and he wasn't making it. One day he spoke with his counselor about it and uncovered in their discussion that he was afraid if he moved into the million-dollar club his buddies, who were very important to him, might not want to be his friend anymore. Once he uncovered the story he was telling himself, he was able to confront his fears and go on to achieve his dream of becoming a million-dollar sales person and keep his friendships.

CHARLOTTE F. LEHECKA, PHD

The lesson here is that since the Universe is always for us, if we are not achieving our heart's desires, we need to ask: "God, show me what's in the way?" "What am I doing or not doing that is blocking my good from coming to me?" And then get quiet and wait. Our prayers are always answered, but we must become quiet or we might miss the response.

As we saw in my story, I had opened the gates to receive at the level of experiencing my regular and ordinary bills getting paid, but not my irregular bills. However, since I now knew that God is the Source of my supply, I simply asked for more. In this case, I asked that I receive the money I needed to pay for an air conditioner, a crown for a tooth and a repair to the overhang on my roof.

Just recently I had another need. The roof on my house was getting old and had sprung a leak at the seam at the bottom of the stairways leading into the living room. So, I let God, the Universe, whatever name you feel most comfortable using, know about this need. Not soon afterward I was talking about needing a new roof with my brother. He shared with me that he had recently had his roof completely replaced because of hail damage. I thought to myself: "Wow, we have had two hail storms this summer. I wonder if I might have hail damage". So I called my home insurance company to ask for an inspection. When the inspector came, he got out of his truck saying: "Don't worry, we are going to take care of this. We are going to get you a new roof". I thought to myself: "Well, I'm not worried, but I am excited to hear you think I might be able to get a new roof"!

He gave me a generous estimate for the roof and the inside repairs. With the monies he gave me, I was not only able to get a new roof, but new gutters and siding AND with the money designated for the inside repairs I was able to negotiate with the contractors to use the money intended to repaint the living room walls which, in my opinion, did not need it to repaint the stairwell ceilings and the upstairs hallway instead—a job I had been wanting to get done for years, but had not believed I had the financial resources available to make these repairs.

Again, I am going into such detail because I want you to experience how God works and your part in the process. What did I have to do? First, I had to be open and receptive, to listen for Spirit's promptings and then act. And I want to tell you, there were a number of potential stumbling blocks for me along the way. They all had to do with my belief system. At each juncture, I had to confront a limiting belief I was telling myself. It was necessary for me to expand my consciousness for the new roof to become a reality.

> False Belief Number 1. I don't have the resources I need to replace my leaking roof.
> False Belief Number 2: It's not okay to accept this supervisor's generosity.

Concerning false belief Number 1, I had to remember that God is the Source of my supply, not me. And God's supply is limitless. To release False belief Number 2, I had to let go of my belief that I am not worthy enough to receive such a gift. As we have talked about before, these beliefs are not necessarily operating at the conscious level; therefore, we must practice awareness—awareness of the messages we give ourselves and choose to change them. One of the tools we have already explored can help when you find yourself "shoulding" on yourself. Do you remember the practice? Yes, it's the Inquiry process by Byron Katie we learned about in Chapter Two.

In addition to tithing, I have discovered that there are basically two kinds of requests of the Universe we can make to create a sense of abundance in our lives: 1) ones we simply put out there as a wonderment with no negative energy attached, and 2) the kinds of requests that align with our life vision, mission and values. We are now going to look at three practices that help us expand our consciousness. The first practice I call the Practice of Wonderment. The second practice is the Practice of Visualization. The third practice is the Practice of Gratitude.

In Chapter Two we used the Visioning Process to determine our Life Purpose, so in this chapter, we want to examine how we are applying our

Divinely Inspired Life Purpose to inform our lives in those areas we have determined are important to us.

The Practice of Wonderment

This practice goes something like this:

*Wouldn't it be wonderful if*_____ (you fill in the blank)

*Wouldn't it be great if*_____(this happened).

In both of these cases the blank is filled in with a heart's desire you have, but one you don't have any negative energy around. It's a desire you hold lightly. You simply put it out there and basically forget all about it. Then, one day, it happens, and you recall: "Oh, yes, I remember putting that desire out to the Universe."

Although I had been practicing this before I read about it without really realizing it was a practice, I was pleased to discover this process described in *Ask and It Is Given: Learning to Manifest Your Desires* by Esther and Jerry Hicks.[5]

In their book they point out the difference in how we present the thought to Universal energy. If we desperately want something to happen that hasn't yet happened, we are putting the thought out there with a *must have* energy. When we do that, we are contaminating the desire with the energy of the absence of that desire. But when we say, "Wouldn't it be great if this desire would come to me?", a very different sort of expectation is created. Our question naturally elicits from us a more positive, expectant response—an expectation which is much less resistant to the natural flow of the universe. When we are being soft and easy about it, when it's not the end of the world for us if it doesn't manifest within the next few hours or days or weeks, we have a much better chance of manifesting our desire.

I have observed that when I use this technique things sometimes manifest really, really quickly. And I'm amazed, and yet I also know better than to start expecting that this will be the case. It's much better to just simply remain pleasantly surprised when we make the connection between the asking and the receiving.

Let me give you an example. When I was in graduate school, I had a friend who just loved his job. I remember saying to myself: "Someday, I want to have work that I love as much as he loves his work". That was it.

Seven years passed and during that time I had work I really, really enjoyed. But when I got to the University of Houston, I learned about a teaching methodology called Accelerated Learning. I knew I had found my passion. And then I remembered that "Wouldn't it be wonderful" … statement I had put out to the universe lo those many years ago.

This process will also help us let in the things we've been asking for in different areas of our life. Below are some examples I have taken from the Hicks book to stimulate our creativity.

> *Wouldn't it be wonderful if we had the best time we have ever had with these friends?*
>
> *Wouldn't it be nice if the traffic is light and we have a wonderful trip?*
>
> *Wouldn't it be nice if I find the most spectacular partner who adores me in the same way I adore him?*
>
> *Wouldn't it be nice if my physical body came into alignment with my dream?*
>
> *Wouldn't it be wonderful if my ideas about food came into alignment so that I find myself taking absolute pleasure from foods that are really in vibrational harmony with what my body needs and wants?* [6]

If you have been obsessing about a particular issue for some time and find it challenging to not think about it—whatever **it** is—then playing this game is a positive alternative. Because, by softly playing this game, what happens is that you hold yourself in a place of alignment. Or alternatively, if you are sick and tired of thinking about a subject, it's also good to let it go, completely.

The Universe already knows our desires even before we express them. So, just let it go, and trust that the Universe which is always working for our good has got this. There is an orchestration that is taking place in response to our request and it will come into alignment for us at the proper time— just trust the process and let it go!!!

The Practice of Visualization

Our life is what our thoughts make it.
Marcus Aurelius

Before we jump into the practice of visualization, we need to back up and first remind ourselves who we truly are and what our unique divine purpose is. Only after we have done the visioning work, does the practice of visualization make any real sense. And it's also important to note that by doing this work, we will not only have a happier, healthier, wiser and more abundant life, we will "consciously" be doing our unique part in making this world a more loving place.

The soul has a two-fold purpose 1) its universal purpose is to rediscover itself as unconditional love, and 2) its individual purpose is to discover and express its unique mission during this life time. When we are connected to Source, we are able to express both our universal and our individual purpose.

Many of us live our lives going through the motions of living without really investing our whole selves in our lives. It's time to change that. Visualization is a powerful manifestation skill. When we visualize ourselves experiencing something, our visualization sets the Universe into motion to manifest our vision into our lives. By visualizing we write the record of our receipt in our subconscious.

So, let's begin with where you are right now. Take some time to get yourself in an empowered state and ask yourself: If I could start with a clean slate in every area of my life, how would I want to show up financially, health-wise, in relationship, in my creative expressions and in my spiritual life? What would I love, love, love to see in my life? What do I yearn for?

You will recall that in Chapter Two we made a list of the different areas in our lives that were important to us. It is time for us to revisit that exercise and expand upon it. With our Divine Purpose Statement in front of us, let's ask ourselves once again how did we score ourselves in each of our areas on the Wheel of Life? For example, my wheel of life includes: life work, financial security, health, family/friends, significant other, community, spiritual life, recreation/fun, home environment, balance. Using a scale from 1-10 with 1 = unsatisfactory to 10=great, I rated each category on the degree to which I am satisfied and fulfilled in that area and plotted it on my wheel of life.

A wheel of life is a wheel with spokes that radiate out from the center. Each spoke has 10 hash lines representing 1-10 and on each spoke we write one of our categories. I then connected all of the dots together which gave me a visual of the gap between where I am and where I would like to be in each of the different areas in my life that are important to me. Now, let's have everyone complete this exercise, or, if you have already completed it, review your answers and plot them on the wheel so you also have a visual presentation of where you are.

Next pick one area you would like to work on by centering and asking yourself: "How does my uniqueness want to be expressed in this area of my life?" Spend time brainstorming, knowing that in the realm of supply, all things are possible. Make sure your sentences are written in the present tense. Specifically describe what you love—only including what you truly want, not what you think you should or could be, have or do. If you want, go back to Chapter Two and reread what you wrote. Perhaps you'll want to add to or tweak your earlier responses.

I am so happy and grateful now that (financial)….

_____

_____.

I am so happy and grateful now that (health)…

_____

_____.

I am so happy and grateful now that (relationships)…

_____

_____.

I am so happy and grateful now that (creative expression)…

_____

_____.

I am so happy and grateful now that (spiritual life)…

_____

_____.

I am so happy and grateful now that (fill in the blank)…

_____

_____.

Add as many lines as you need to capture all the elements on your wheel. Then after you have read my examples below, go back to your purpose statement and make sure you have captured the essence of who you are and how you came here to serve. You may find it helpful to do as I have done and write definitions for each of your values too. It's oh, so important that this NOT be just another exercise, but that your life purpose statement be your daily compass guiding all the decisions you make in all areas of your life. In a short while, you will learn to read your heart's guidance as you notice your body's response to certain ideas and by listening to your intuition.

Hopefully, my stories will bring this activity to life for you. But first, let me share my vision, values and mission statement. Then, we can see how those values act as a North Star in our life—keeping us in alignment with our overarching individual life purpose and informing our specific mission in each of the areas represented on the wheel.

Vision: A spiritually awakened world in which all people live in joyful gratitude.

When I read this vision, I am uplifted. My heart soars. It has never become mundane. Each time I hear, see and feel these words, I am inspired.

Values: Kindness, Learner, Committed, Creative, Mindful, Futuristic, Connectedness

Kindness—There is this bulletin board at church with all kinds of different sayings related to kindness I never tire of reading. Here are some of the sayings:

> *Every act of love and kindness raises the vibration of the entire Universe.*
> *The highest form of wisdom is kindness.*—Talmud
> *No act of kindness, however small, is ever wasted.*—Aesop
> *Act with kindness, do not expect gratitude.*—Confucius
> *Be kind to unkind people. They need it the most.*
> *Kindness is a language the deaf can hear and the blind can see.*—M. Twain

Learner—Being a learner is in my DNA as the two examples below will make clear. Being a learner is more than learning, however, it is in learning and sharing my learning that I am able to be of service to others.

Committed—Making and keeping commitments as well as being 100% committed to any activity I take on is the outgrowth of my making a point to choose to commit to those things I am also passionate about.

Creative—One of the reasons I have enjoyed learning and practicing Accelerated Learning is because it requires so much creativity. As a practitioner, we must write stories, create songs, act out skits, read to music, create posters, etc. And because I know that learners with whom I interact have varied learning styles, it's important that I create and deliver programs that address the learning needs of all of the learners.

Mindful—Mindfulness is in the moment awareness, a practice I do my best to live into each day. When I do I know that I am living from my Christ Consciousness in my interactions with others.

Futuristic—My mind enjoys imagining how things might be. This entire book is filled with my imaginings of how we might live, interact and move toward a world in which all people live in joyful gratitude.

Connectedness—It speaks to my belief that things happen for a reason. There is a divine plan, and we are a part of it—of something larger than ourselves. This feeling of connectedness carries certain responsibilities with it. If we are all part of a larger picture, then we must not harm others (this includes our Earth and all of its inhabitants) because we will be harming ourselves.

Mission: My mission may be different in each of the areas of my life on my wheel, but it will be infused by my vision and my values.

Current Professional Life Mission: To be a catalyst in moving others toward a more awakened state of being in the world through writing, consulting, teaching, speaking and mindfully interacting with others of all ages, backgrounds and cultures.

Can you now imagine how I might live out each of my values while fulfilling my mission to be a catalyst for change? Can you imagine how you might live out your values while living out your mission?

I believe we are called to be of service and that this happens where our deepest desires and the needs of the world intersect. My first story is about **the learner** in me recognizing that it was time to move on. I had been at the University of Houston for 17 years and I loved my work, yet I was also experiencing what I call "divine discontent". I was being called to something more. I wanted to be able to bring these Accelerated Learning (AL) principles about which I was so passionate to a wider audience. I wanted to expose not only teachers, but also school principles to this amazing teaching methodology which I believe honors each learner.

Sometimes pursuing our dreams means we also have to give up something. For me, that meant giving up my job at the UH to pursue a doctorate in education. I had been going to a nearby University part-time, but that wasn't satisfying. Both because I am **a learner** and because **commitment** is an important value for me. I wanted to be able to put my whole self into this process so I made the decision to commit full-time to my education and to return to a part of the country where I felt a strong **connection** to the environment.

I was **mindful** that my children were not particularly happy about my decision to move and although I wanted to support them in whatever way I could, this new life direction had such a strong pull on me that I literally felt like I would die spiritually if I did not follow this soul call. So, I applied and was accepted at the University of North Carolina in Greensboro (UNCG).

In the Prose section of this chapter Murray explained what happens when we make a decision that aligns with our vision, mission and values. He talked about how—when we follow our calling—the Universe supports us in what seem like miraculous ways. The following story is just such an example of how the universe literally lines up to support you on your journey. There were a couple of snags, but there was this knowing that this is what I'm to do, so I kept my focus.

When I initially applied for UNCG's doctoral program in Curriculum and Instruction, I found out I had been accepted but that the college had put my start date in the wrong semester. By the time this was sorted out, there were no more scholarships available and I needed a scholarship to attend.

I was doing an AL teacher training for teachers in Princeton, NJ when the call came. It appeared that one of the students who had been accepted into the program was not able to leave her country: Did I still want to come in the fall, and did I still want a scholarship? I said "yes" to both.

When I returned home, I had three weeks to sell my home and pack for the journey. I did an open house for two weekends which was all of the time I had. On the morning of my departure, a couple came by, said they wanted to buy the house, and would I be okay with a cash payment? Would I?

Once we arrived, I got my special needs daughter settled immediately into her new placement, but since my son and I had no place to stay, we lived in our pop-up tent camper for six weeks until we found a home to buy and I could close on the house in Texas. That time turned out to be a very special bonding time with one another.

The second story is similar in that it also demonstrates what can happen when we set an intention or create a visualization. Once again, the Universe puts opportunities in our path.

Another of my passions is protecting our environment. I had just completed a 13 once-a-week evening course which opened my eyes to what is happening to our environment when I received this catalogue in the mail from the Omega Institute. I have been on their mailing list since my days at UH and I loved looking at all of their course offerings, but each time I would say to myself, "that sounds great, but" …but mainly I didn't have the money for these courses, at least, that was what I would tell myself.

Then my eyes fell upon this six-week course offering entitled: *Ecological Literacy Certification Program.* My heart started pounding. My eyes lit up. Oh, wow! This sounds wonderful. I knew this was something for me. Whereas before, I had been in a poverty consciousness mind-set about all of the other courses, all of a sudden I believed there had to be a way for me to participate in this program. That shift in consciousness is all-important because it is our guidance system letting us know what's really important to each of us. None of the other programs—although exciting—had my name written on it. Just this one. And when your name is written on something, then everything falls into place for it to become a part of your new reality.

I called them just to get some more information—thinking that maybe the following year I could apply. I already had a commitment I could not get out of during the middle of this course and couldn't imagine them letting me take it if I were going to have to miss two weeks. But I was wrong! The person with whom I spoke encouraged me to come and even told me about scholarships they had available.

As you can imagine, I applied for one, was accepted and was able to take the course for a third of the cost. I figured out it was probably less expensive for me to be there than if I had been at home during that same time! Since the course extended over such a long time period, we were required to live in a tent, but we got three squares of some of the best food you can imagine each day. And as it turned out, tent-living was heaven! And not only that, the two weeks I missed were on permaculture—a subject I was really interested in, but also knew I could take from a renowned permaculturist who lived in Greensboro. And I did the next year!!!

As both of these stories testify, living a rich life is about more than money. Therefore, let's ask ourselves the following questions concerning your vision for one of the areas on your wheel. Take each desire that you have written for each of your categories and ask yourself the following questions of each desire:

Ask within: What do I want? Ask that question over and over again until you are able to discern your deepest "why".

Ask within: What is the highest ideal this will satisfy?

Ask within: What will I feel emotionally if this ideal is satisfied?

Once you have completed this process for each of your heart's desires in a specific category, review what you have written and check yourself to make certain it demonstrates

- Clarity
- High purpose
- Coming from love
- In our and everyone's best interest

Then take a deep breath and congratulate yourself. You have done some powerful work and your life will thank you for it. Take a break and when you are ready take each of your deepest desires in each category through this process.

We know the power of our word. Our last step in this process is to take each of our categories and write affirmative statements for each. We examined Affirmative Statements in Chapter One, but to review: Affirmative statements need to be written in the present tense. They are clear, straight-forward statements of positive change in body, being and performance. They focus our best conscious efforts on transformation while seeking to enlist powers beyond our conscious understanding.

For example: Say you're a person who is often too busy or preoccupied to consider other people's feelings. You want to develop more empathy. Your affirmation could be "I enjoy a profound empathy for other people that sometimes appears to be telepathic." While this may seem like a denial of reality, it's really an instrument for creating a parallel, present tense reality in your consciousness. It allows you to access one of the many possible realities available to us when we make the conscious demand or ask of the Universe.

Sometimes, I find it helpful to create affirmations that are playful in nature—especially if it's a hard sell to my conscious mind. Let me give you an example from Edwene Gaines that I just love. And since this chapter's focus has been mainly on financial abundance, this affirmation is completely apropos:

LARGE, RICH, OPULENT, LAVISH FINANCIAL SURPRISES
COME TO ME NOW AND I AM GRATEFUL!!!

Practice: The Law of Gratitude

Meister Eckhart, a German theologian, is credited with saying: "If the only prayer you ever say in your entire life is 'thank you', it will be enough." [7] I could not agree with him more. I begin each day—even before I get out of bed—thanking God. "Thank you God, for this day. Thank you for my health, thank you for my toes, thank you for my body. Thank you for…. Thank you, thank you, thank you!" I must say this phrase hundreds of times each day. It never gets old. Instead, it is my constant recognition and acknowledgment throughout the day of God's help, God's love, God's grace.

I encourage each of you as you go through your day, just say "thank you" for every little thing. It keeps your spirits lifted and your heart wide open, appreciative, and full of gratitude. It puts a smile on your face. It creates a bubbling up of "happiness" inside of you. It puts bounce in your step and a praise-filled heart ready to burst forth in song at a moment's notice. There is nothing like it. Nothing!!! And because "Gratitude" supports the Law of Attraction, creating and sustaining a high vibration throughout the day draws to you automatically other people, places and events operating at your same frequency. This is the abundantly-filled life we all seek for ourselves and others.

CHARLOTTE F. LEHECKA, PHD

SIX

VIBRATING WITH HEALTH:
NO MATTER WHAT THE AILMENT,
LOVE IS THE CURE

Prose

Prayer is not a duty or a habit,
But pouring forth of the heart in gratitude
For every breath, every moment of life...

Sue Sikking

So, what does it mean to vibrate with health? It's a question I have wrestled with for many years. In my own personal life, physical health is not something I have given a lot of conscious attention. I've heard it said that oftentimes people born into wealth just expect to have prosperous lives; they never question it. It's simply an unwritten law of their consciousness and because that is their expectation, that is their experience. So it is, I believe, with my health.

As I mentioned earlier in the book, I grew up in a small town in Mississippi. Although we lived in town we had five acres, two of which were farmed and two were used to graze cows and raise pigs and chickens. We would pick and freeze the vegetables each year and store them in one of our two freezers. Then, once every two years, we refreshed our meat supply by slaughtering a calf and a pig. The only food supplements we bought from the grocery store were the basics—bread, flour, sugar, salt, pepper and lard.

I have always attributed my good health and those of my family to that healthy start we got in life. Of course, one could argue the validity of my assumptions, but as we have been learning throughout this book, our beliefs create our reality. I have just simply grown up not questioning my right to be "healthy".

That is not to say that there have been no health challenges in my life. Once, a long time ago, I was walking the beach in Galveston with a friend of mine and I stepped on a Man-of-War sting ray. Talking about pain—childbirth did not hold a candle to this kind of pain. It was the kind that literally takes your breath away.

I remember her looking for help along the beach, and finding none, she took me back to the car where she laid me down and helped me practice breathing. She talked to me in a soothing voice, helping me to calm down and breathe—deep, slow breaths. As I became more and more relaxed, I noticed that the pain subsided more and more. It felt almost magical. Just relax and watch the pain go away.

Since then, I have used this technique many times to put myself in an altered state by slowing my brain wave frequency from beta to theta. In this altered state which I also describe as my meditative state where I am able to experience Oneness with the ALL, any pain I might be experiencing the moment before—be it physical, mental or emotional—simply goes away. In that state my awareness of being a physical body having a human experience simply disappears. I still know that I am me and yet my "me" has expanded so that it takes in the allness of everything.

I also experienced another health challenge. About twenty-five years ago, I went to a dermatologist about a bump on my face that just wouldn't go away. When I learned it was cancerous, I was scared to death and quickly had it removed. However, since I have come to believe that any illness is actually a sign of an imbalance in our lives, upon reflection I was able to thank the cancer for giving me a warning sign, apologize to my body for having to endure my lack of willingness to listen earlier and discover what I needed to do.

At that time, I was working 70-hour weeks and not spending any time with my family or taking care of myself as I should. It had taken a cancerous growth on my face which had to be cut out for the Universe to get my attention. It worked. I immediately took a three-month Sabbatical. During this time, I did things that nourished my spirit. I refinished an oak table I loved, I sorted hundreds of pictures and lovingly placed them in picture albums which I still enjoy perusing and sharing with others. And I planted a garden. I also took the time to participate in my children's school events. It was wonderful. And when I was ready to go back to work, I cut my hours to ¾ time, so that I would be able to continue to enjoy time with my children.

Knowing we can move from a state of pain to a state of no pain and that we can facilitate a healing simply by exorcising our belief and expectation of illness really brings home the message of the awesome power we humans have to create and recreate our own reality. If I start to doubt this reality, I simply remind myself of the true story of Eve betrayed in the movie, *The Three Faces of Eve*. In this movie, Eve has three different personalities. In one of the personalities, she needed glasses to see; in another, she had perfect vision.

Our race consciousness teaches us that with age comes poorer health although the facts would suggest otherwise. According to Deepak Chopra,[1] our bodies are constantly renewing themselves so that literally every part is made new within a seven-year cycle.

When I read this many years ago, I claimed this as truth for me. In recent years, as I have moved more and more from a survival mode to a thrival mode of living, my health has continued to improve. When people ask me what my secret to such good health is, I tell them that as I age, I get wiser. By this I mean I work every day to become more conscious of my mental and emotional patterns and to change them into more life affirming thoughts and feelings. When I create new awarenesses of wholeness, I change my beliefs and when I change my beliefs, I banish the disease patterns at the quantum level—a level beyond the tissues, the cells and even the atoms—a level known only in the silent empty spaces beyond all physical matter.

I have a body, but I am not my body. I am the observer of my body. That observer whom I refer to as my Higher Consciousness speaks to me through my heart and gently lets me know when I am off track and guides me to what I need to do to get back on track.

Though my health has continued to improve, my heart goes out to the many people I meet who are not yet enjoying good health. So, I made another request of the universe. I asked to be shown a method of healing that was so simple even a child could do it.

Several years later, through a treatment modality called *Reconnective Healing*,[2] I experienced a healing that came about through allowing my body to be a conduit for the healing energies that surround us all of the time, but which sometimes only become available to us when we understand our bodies are like antennas. Just like we must turn on the radio to a specific channel if we want to capture the radio waves floating around in the atmosphere, we must do the same with our bodies. We must consciously invite the healing energies into our physical bodies in order to precipitate a healing.

Let me share my first experience with "energy" healing or "spiritual" healing. Out of the blue I had some growths appear on my back. Now, because of the cancer scare earlier in my life, at first I panicked. Soon, though I was able to become calm thanks to my meditation practice and my core belief that at my source, I am whole, I am health.

I reasoned; I have this incredible opportunity to prove to myself whether *Reconnective Healing* works, and if it doesn't I can always go to the doctor and have the growth removed just like I had the cancer on my face removed. But, if it did work, then I would be aware of at least one very simple treatment modality that one could use to help

CHARLOTTE F. LEHECKA, PHD

people who were without health care and yet in need of a healing. As you have probably guessed, it obviously worked or I would not be sharing.

I had a friend who was keeping an eye on this growth for me as it was challenging for me to see it very well since it was on my back. It kept growing and growing and really looked ugly. Then, one day, about a week after I had practiced the treatment on myself, she commented that it was looking worse and that it was becoming brown. While she had seen that as a negative, I thought "brown" that's actually a "good sign" because that means it is no longer getting a blood supply." And I was right. But the actual moment of truth came a few days later.

I had reached back to touch it to see how it was doing and I inadvertently touched the incorrect spot. It's important to note that I thought I had touched the actual spot. Thinking so, I experienced what I would call "unqualified joy". About 10 seconds after that, I reached back again and discovered I had not touched the correct spot, but it was too late. I had already experienced it gone and that experience was so powerful that nothing—not even feeling the spot and knowing it was actually still there—could take away from that experience. In that moment, I had what I have described throughout this book as a "knowing" and within a matter of days, the growth simply sloughed off my body.

More recently, having recognized the exponential power of praying in one accord, I have been serving as a prayer chaplain and participating in two healing intention groups. So, what do I mean by "praying in one accord"? For me, it's all about connecting—connecting with one another and connecting with our source.

My first experience of this "power of one accord" began when I became a prayer chaplain. I discovered that when we pray together, there is a shift that takes place. Suddenly, I become connected to a source beyond me. You may think when you ask a prayer chaplain to pray with you that the prayer chaplain is the giver and you are the receiver, BUT that is simply NOT TRUE. <u>Both</u> are givers and receivers.

As prayer chaplains we are to listen empathically, connecting with what's alive in the other person—making no judgements. Our goal is simply to hear what's alive in you and what you would like. And then hold that for you.

When the person asking for prayer makes themselves vulnerable by sharing what's alive in them, this is a "gift". In that moment—in that "Holy instant", we are connected in an extraordinary way. It is as if our hearts are wired to a bigger network. And as a prayer chaplain, words simply pour out with no conscious thought of my own. There's just something that happens when we make a conscious decision to share "unconditional love" with another that is greater than either of us. It is the power of ONE ACCORD.

Many of the references in the Bible about the apostles being "of one accord" mention an act of group healing. In Luke 9:1, Jesus gave his apostles "power and authority"…to cure diseases". St. Mathew in Mathew 4:23 also noted that the multitudes would bring the sick folks and that they were healed EVERYONE.

And what was the 12 disciples' method of group prayer? It was to be "with one mind and one passion." The scripture emphasizes that the apostles were to pray as a passionate unity with a single voice. The gospel of Luke shares over and over again that what they did, THEY DID TOGETHER. All of them united and unanimous.

In my two modern-day intention groups, this is also what we do. The words may be more up-to-date, but the goal is the same: One of us asks our group to hold an intention for us and as a group we sit in the Silence for fifteen minutes and do just that. We believe as the apostles did that our united voices can and do make a difference. What our groups have discovered is that not only do our prayers make a difference in the life of those for whom we pray, but because that healing energy must pass through us, we benefit as well.

Principle

As these vignettes from my life point out, our essence is wholeness. And when we are experiencing anything less than wholeness, our lives are out of balance in some way. There are many different avenues available to us to restore our health from healthy, nutritional eating and exercise to traditional or alternative healing treatments. In this book, our practices focus on our Core Teaching Four, the power of meditative prayer as a healing modality.

Our Essence is Wholeness

My experience of wholeness has helped me to realize that at our core, our essence, we are all perfect, all whole. Imagine, since we are all energy beings, that at our essence we are this beautiful white light—pure and bright, shining in all our glory. Then, imagine that because of false beliefs we have entertained about ourselves, our white light has become crusted over. The light is still there; we have just hidden it under a bushel as the song goes. Our job in this lifetime is to simply remember who we are—to remove all those limitations—to remove the bushel so our light can shine again.

I have also come to believe that no matter what the ailment—whether it's physical, emotional, mental, or spiritual—**love is the cure**. That cure can come through many different forms. If you believe in traditional medicine, then going to a doctor for help is you loving yourself. If you believe in alternative methods of treatment, then seeking out solutions in that arena for help is you loving yourself. If you believe that prayer is the answer, then going into the Silence for help is you loving yourself. For a long time, I was puzzled how such diverse methods could each bring about a cure for the same disease. All three work as long as—at the same time—we recognize that ALL illness of any kind is really only an expression of our disconnect from our Source, PURE LOVE.

What each of these three different roads to health has in common is a shift in awareness in the person. When we truly believe in the efficacy of any method to effect a positive change, we have learned that this belief alone is what makes the shift possible. Think about the example from my story. When I touched the spot on my back and thought it gone, that conviction was so strong that the actual physical manifestation of the spot had no power. That exemplified a change in my belief pattern at the most basic level of existence. A new awareness emerged; I believed a cure was possible. It also made it absolutely clear to me that we have the power to change the pattern. Just that awareness alone brings about new faith, lays down a new track in our consciousness, and the physical body has no other option than to follow it into wholeness.

On our path, we make many discoveries and have many "aha" moments. When it comes to healing, I have been especially influenced by the work of Louise Hay, Myrtle Fillmore's healing story, the work of Hugh Lin, a psychiatrist who lives and works in Hawaii who healed psychiatric patients whom he never actually saw using the Hawaiian prayer Ho'Oponopono, the work of the Heart-Math Institute and Lynn McTaggart's Power of Eight Intention groups. As we look at the way to health through prayer, I will be sharing each of their practices with you.

Practice: Using Affirmative (Affirmations and Denials) Prayer to heal ourselves and others.

Affirmative Prayer: Anytime I or someone else for whom I'm praying is expressing a disconnect from Source which can show up as an ailment in the physical body, I immediately grab my Louise Hay book, *Heal Your Body: the Mental Causes for Physical Illness and the Metaphysical Way to Overcome Them*, to discover what the specific block to expressing perfect health might be and I imagine that block—be it resentment, anger, deep-seated hurt—whatever it is dissolving and love coming in to fill the space. My specific practice is to create a positive affirmation for a specific healing. Sometimes, I also combine both denials and affirmations when setting my intention.

Let's say for example, a person is having sinus issues. According to Louise Hay [3], sinus issues from a metaphysical perspective represent an irritation to one person, someone close. The antidote is "I declare peace and harmony indwell me and surround me at all times. All is well."

When I read Hay's metaphysical interpretations, I find for the most part that they are spot on. However, there are times when I am personally not able to relate to the diagnosis, yet I know I am experiencing the condition in my physical body. I then stop—get quiet—go inside and ask to be shown exactly what needs to be released or forgiven. And then I wait for guidance. Once, I am given an insight, I practice denials and affirmations which we learned about in Chapter One around what I have been given. The following is an example:

> I let go of the tension in my neck and shoulders.
> I recognize the tension comes from my feeling overwhelmed.
> I have all the time I need to do the things that are mine to do.
> I am always in the right place at the right time.
> My whole life is in harmony and divine order.

The key in creating affirmations isn't just to write them and say them, it is to "feel" them too. So, I recommend picking out a phrase that resonates with you and just keep saying it over and over again or putting the phrase somewhere you will see it often, read it and connect with it at your soul level.

Practice: Myrtle Fillmore's Healing Method

A second practice I use to bless my physical body comes from Myrtle Fillmore, co-founder with her husband, Charles Fillmore of the Unity movement. As a child Myrtle had been told she had inherited tuberculosis from her parents and that she was born to be ill, suffer and die early. As a young adult, Myrtle did contract tuberculosis and experienced a flare up complicated by the fevers of malaria. Ultimately, the doctors told her they could do nothing else for her and that the end of her life was near.

Myrtle, clutching at any straw, attended a lecture given by Dr. E.B. Weeks, who was a metaphysician. During the lecture, Dr. Weeks uttered one sentence that spoke directly to Myrtle's soul. It was "I am a child of God and, therefore, I do not inherit sickness." [4] She knew she had been given the tool she needed to heal herself. Myrtle shared her process of healing in an article entitled: "How I Found Health." Here is an excerpt from that pamphlet.

> ...I was thinking about life. ...Then it flashed upon me that I might talk to the life in every part of my body and have it do just what I wanted. I began to teach my body and got wonderful results. I told the life in my liver that it was not torpid or inert, but full of vigor and energy. I told the life in my stomach that it was not weak or inefficient, but energetic, strong, and intelligent. I told the life in my abdomen that it was no longer infested with ignorant ideas of disease, put there by myself and by doctors, but that it was all athrill with the sweet, pure, wholesome energy of God. I told my limbs that they were active and strong. I told my eyes that they did not see of themselves but that they expressed the sight of Spirit, and that they were drawing on an unlimited source.

> I went to all of the life centers of my body and spoke words of Truth to them—words of strength and power. I asked their forgiveness for the foolish, ignorant course I had pursued in the past, when I had condemned them and called them weak, inefficient and diseased. ...I told them that they were no longer in bondage to the carnal mind, that they were not corruptible flesh, but centers of life and energy omnipresent.

> Then I asked the Father to forgive me for taking His life into my organism and there using it so meanly. I promised God that I would never, ever again retard the free flow of that life through my mind and my body by any false word or thought; that I would always bless it and encourage it with true thoughts and words.

CHARLOTTE F. LEHECKA, PHD

I also saw that I was using the life of the Father in thinking thoughts and speaking words, and I became very watchful as to what I thought and said. I did not let any worried or anxious thoughts into my mind, and I stopped speaking gossipy, frivolous, angry words. I let a little prayer go up every hour that Jesus Christ would be with me and help me to think and speak only kind, loving, true words. (6)

From the time Myrtle began this practice until she was completely healed took about two years. Myrtle lived to be 87. About a year before she made her transition, she began to intuit it was time for her to continue her work on the other side. A couple of weeks before her death, she began saying her good-byes, letting the people closest to her know it was time for her to go. On the evening before she made her transition, she was seen climbing a ladder and picking apples from their apple orchard. She went to bed and died in her sleep.

What I love most about this story is not only that Myrtle was able to heal herself, but that she also knew when it was time to lay down this human form and cross over into the realm of spirit. For me, this is a model of what is possible—not only for me, but for all of us. We can choose health and we can decide when our work here is done and leave without experiencing physical discomfort of any kind.

In my own practice, I take time each day to send love to each part of my body. I start with my feet and I work my way up, seeing each cell in my body radiating pure love and knowing that pure love **must** manifest as a healthy, physical body.

Practice: Ho'Oponopono Prayer

One of the biggest blocks to health of every kind is unforgiveness. It affects our physical health, our relationship health, our financial health—our actually everything! In Edwene Gaines's book, *The Four Spiritual Laws of Prosperity*, Forgiveness is her Spiritual Law 3. She says: "Freeing yourself from judging others is a step in learning what you truly want out of life."(6)

Gary Simmons in his book, *I of the Storm*, describes "forgiveness" as reconciliation.[7] I really like his use of this term because I happen to believe that many of us have gotten the wrong impression of what forgiveness truly is. My own personal word for "forgiveness" is reconnection as I shared in Chapter Three.

In his book, *Radical Forgiveness*, Colin Tipping says that there really is nothing to forgive—ever! [8] Understood rightly, I agree with him. My minister used to ask when I would talk to her—or more appropriately—complain to her about something that was going on in my life: "What if nothing is wrong in this situation?" This would cause me to ponder: "If nothing and no one is ever against us, if this universe is always for us," then how am I to understand what's going on? If I look to Core Teachings 1 and 2, which say that God is everywhere present and always good and we are made of God stuff, how does that shift my perception of the situation and my sense of connection to all others? The Ho'Oponopono prayer [9] has been a real help in shifting my consciousness from one of judgment or a poor me attitude to one of connection. The prayer is very simple:

> I apologize. (I'm sorry=original version).
> Please forgive me.
> Thank you.
> I love you.

When I was first introduced to this prayer I had some resistance because I was thinking: "If there is nothing to forgive, then why am I saying, 'I'm sorry, please forgive me'." My second resistance was to the use of the word "sorry" after the word "I". I have been taught to be very careful about any word I put after the word "I". Since I do not want to affirm "I am sorry", I changed the words to "I apologize". Once I substituted "I apologize" for the words "I am sorry" and began working with this prayer saying, "I apologize, please forgive me", it has taken on a whole new meaning.

When I say "I apologize, please forgive me" it is my recognition that I am a part of this collective whole and since every thought I have either adds to the health and wholeness of the whole or detracts from it, I want to take responsibility for any part I have played—consciously or unconsciously—in fueling our individual and collective sense of separation from Wholeness.

When I say "thank you", it is me thanking Me for the willingness to restore Wholeness. And when I say, "I love you", it's me reconciling myself to Myself.

This may sound a bit esoteric to you, yet I encourage you—let go of trying to wrap your head around it and go straight to the heart, for it is there you will feel the shift toward reconciliation whether it be between you and another or you and a part of your body.

Once the reconciliation takes place within us, we usually experience one of two things, the situation shifts in a positive direction or, we shift in such a way that though the same thing may be happening in the outer, we do not feel diminished by it. We have re-established our Wholeness and are coming from our center in our interactions with ourselves and others.

Practice: Heart-Math Prayer

The HeartMath Institute is an organization dedicated to restoring peace and balance on the planet. I have one prayer in particular I want to introduce. They call it The Quick Coherence Technique [10]. What I love about this prayer or technique if you prefer to see it that way is its versatility. We can use it to strengthen the attributes of the heart, such as love, appreciation, care and compassion. By breathing in these qualities of the heart and imprinting them on our intentions for health, we shift the energy to a higher, more wholistic level.

The Quick Coherence technique is what I call an in-the-moment prayer and can be used throughout our day. All you do is: STOP! Breathe in and out through the heart! Call to mind a person, animal, situation that causes you to feel unconditional love and take in that feeling fully. It can be especially useful for the following:

- To restore balance and flow when feeling stressed or overloaded;

- During transitions, such as before a meeting, before going into work or coming home;
- Before important communication, such as phone calls, emails, or speaking to someone about a problem;
- Before beginning our Power of Eight Intention group prayer.

Practice: Power of Eight Intention Group

The quick coherence technique is what the members of my Power of Eight Intention group use as our way to prepare ourselves before we actually begin holding the specific evening affirmation. I have been a part of a Power of Eight Intention group for a little over two years now. I love the way McTaggart puts it. She says: "When people are involved in a passionate activity like a healing circle, they transmute from a solitary voice into a thunderous symphony." [11]

Our thunderous symphony meets every Sunday and Wednesday evening via text messaging at 9:15 PM. At each meeting, we focus on the prayer intention of one of our group members. Once we know what the prayer intention is, we use the Quick Coherence protocol to establish the optimal heart space for our time together.

Quick Coherence—Use to restore balance and flow and to strengthen the attributes of the heart, i.e. love, appreciation, care and compassion

    a. Focus on heart
    b. heart-focused breathing (i.e. imagine breathing in and out of the heart)
    c. while doing heart-based breathing, focus on some powerful positive image as you breathe—one that taps you into unconditional love [12]

Then, for 15 minutes we all focus on the same intention. At the end of our time, we often share what came to us during the intending process. Never before have I ever had visual images when praying, but from the very beginning of our time together, I receive vivid images related to the prayer intention our group is holding. What's also really interesting is that when we compare the different images we each held, many, many times they are almost identical.

Sometimes, I have gone into this experience with a headache or feeling out of sorts for one reason or another, but by the end of this time—this 15 minutes—, I am a changed person. A sense of peace permeates my very being.

And what of the person for whom we have intended? I can only speak of what it's been like for me to be on the receiving end of that prayer power. I feel so loved, so supported. My body tingles and I simply float on air for some time after one of our sessions. Some of the unintended benefits I have experienced as a result of our praying together is I notice that, in general, I feel more peaceful and joy-filled than ever before. I find that my bouts with self-pity are rare these days and when they do come, are shorter-lived. Others in our group have also reported a much more expanded state of well-being.

Another really interesting finding in McTaggart's research is—not only what happens when we pray for others—, but what happens to the persons doing the praying. She describes her participants as having entered a state of "unio mystica" or that stage on the spiritual path where the self feels a complete merging with the Absolute.

St Theresa of Avila describes it as "cocooned in divine love"—the moment when all sense of individuality disappears, and you exist in a state of ecstatic union. [13] When I read those words, I thought—"How beautifully they communicate my own experience as a prayer chaplain and as a member of our power of 8 group."

What happens is that the boundary of us/not us becomes blurred. The intention takes over and you feel completely and mystically absorbed into the object of your intention. And—most importantly for all of us, the beauty of this state is that anyone—anyone—you, you and you— we can ALL move into this state effortlessly by holding onto the power of a collective thought. Dr. Charles Tart refers to this state as "cosmic consciousness". [14]

This has certainly been my experience when participating in our World Day of Prayer ceremony, in which we hold an intention for the people from every country on this planet. The space is filled with a surge of compassionate love. There is an overwhelming sense of unity with the other participants and a powerful connection with the people of each country for whom we are holding an intention.

It's bigger than—"it will be good if I do this." It's more like—"we are part of it and it is part of us"—far beyond just engaging in a process. Newberg says that this supports the idea that "a mind can exist without ego, that awareness can exist without self." [15]

In McTaggart's work, one participant wrote, "Besides these feelings of unity, I have felt a strong sense of having been part of a profound and significant effort." Marcia from Mexico City said she felt hopeful, a sense of "human solidarity" and an end to the feelings of isolation. Instead, she felt part of a deep sense of connection. She stated: "I felt a greater sense of purpose than my small life. I felt compelled to do this." [16]

She and others also spoke about the "deep sense of longing" they experienced once their project came to an end. I, too, can identify with this feeling because for a short time, we cut back on our prayer time from 4 days a week to one day a week and we all felt the loss of connection—immediately. We quickly adjusted our plans!!!

McTaggart learned from her participants that one of the side benefits of being a part of these groups of 8 was that praying in a group causes deep, positive, permanent psychological transformation in many participants and improvements in their daily lives.

One of the healing effects had to do with a feeling of global trust—that so rarely experienced sense—that LIFE truly loves us. I can only attest to the fact that since I began this group—my life has been more beautiful.

Also, McTaggart noted that many of her participants experienced the "mirror effect." If they prayed for peace, their lives became more peaceful. If they tried to heal someone else, they experienced a healing in their own lives. One simply said: I *work better when I am in service in this way.* This is also true for me*: I work better when I am in service in this way!*

To sum up, I would like to say that this kind of prayer is essentially a movement of the heart. One participates for no personal gain, but purely from an instinct of love. And for some strange reason, it is in those moments when we are not thinking about ourselves that healings come to us.

So, why pray for others? Well, other than the benefits I just mentioned, there are times when the other person is too close to the situation and cannot see past the burden. It is in those times we can hold the space of "wholeness" for them when they are too upset or scared to rest in divine peace.

Prayer is the energy of our thoughts and feelings and we can direct that energy toward specific outcomes. We can through our focused intention on "wholeness" create an optimum environment for healing to occur. In this way, if a friend or family member has an intention to recover, we can add our energy to the healing process. On the other hand, if our friend or family member has made a soul choice to leave human form, our prayers won't keep them alive. Ultimately, the outcomes are up to each individual's Higher Self. We cannot know the highest and best outcomes for other people. Ours is simply to see them "whole" while releasing the outcome.

Each of us has a highly individualized soul journey while on Earth. Let me share another personal example. I have been blessed with a daughter, Nana, who shortly after her arrival in this world was diagnosed with a syndrome called Prader-Willi. There is a piece missing in the fifteenth chromosome that has all kinds of effects, but the complications that come with obesity is one of the main culprits in shortened life expectancies. Because of this side-effect, we have learned a lot about the care and maintenance of the physical form and have actually become "unrecognized nutritional experts"!!!

In order to maintain her weight, Nana must abide by a very strict nutritional regimen—not some of the time but all of the time. If she eats even the least little thing that is not on her eating plan, she can—just like that—add ten pounds to her weight. Weight that is easy to put on, but not so easy to take off. When you ask her why she is here and what her purpose is, she will tell you that she is here to be an example for other people who have Prader-Willi.

We also both share the belief that she chose to come into this life to hone the art of discipline. Each and every day I am truly amazed at the self-control she must practice. It is not easy. To protect herself from herself, many years ago she requested I put locks on the refrigerator and on the cabinets which I have done. I am in awe of how she can be around others eating all kinds of foods that she cannot have and be content—even find joy—with what she can have.

Nana has been described as mildly mentally retarded, but what I see is a very mature soul with a gift for healing others with her smile and the positive energy she radiates. She has a heart for healing. Just recently, we were having a conversation about past life experiences and she told me matter-of-factly that in her next incarnation she wanted to come back with leukemia. Once again, she wants to be a light for others who have leukemia.

In this Chapter on Radiating Health, we have been talking about how to maintain our health and ways in which we can support others in regaining their health and yet here is someone, who is saying she wants to come into this next life with another disability to serve others who have leukemia. I cried and I also laughingly told her that if she wanted to come back with leukemia, that is, of course, her choice, but she might need to find herself another mother!!!

So, I leave you with the question: "What is wholeness really?"

CHARLOTTE F. LEHECKA, PHD

EPILOGUE

WHERE DO WE GO FROM HERE?

You are worthwhile simply because you are alive.
Never forget this and you're sure to thrive.
Wayne Dyer

True freedom requires that we be awake and aware, and we must choose constantly every day to stay on the right track and avoid slipping back into old ways of thinking and behaving.

I invite you to think of your life as a project that you get to **design and refine**. For me it's helpful to go back to my vision, mission and values statements. There I am reminded what's important to me. As I mentioned earlier in the book, reading my vision statement—*a spiritually awakened world in which all people live in joyful gratitude*—takes my breath away every time.

Sometimes thinking about how I might play a part in addressing this vision can feel overwhelming. The question becomes: Where do I start? What is mine to do? How do I express my purpose? Again, I refer to my values. They portray what I'm passionate about, what brings me joy. When I remind myself that I am first and foremost a learner, that I'm always imagining how things could be and that I am an integral part of the connected whole, my values come alive and give me direction. They motivate me to write a book such as this where I am able to share powerful change-making tools I learned from others and in so doing be of service to others.

Before I sit down to write I say these words to myself or sometimes out loud: *I dedicate this work to my awakening in order that I may serve and awaken all beings.* I close each session with the following words: *I offer the benefits of this work today to the welfare and awakening of all beings.* These two statements keep me humble and remind me that I am an instrument through which God's energy flows.

I want to humbly acknowledge that I am not a finished product and that I'm not really an expert in any of the material I write about in this book. That is why I refer you time and time again to the authors from whom I drew wisdom who have made a difference in my life. I have laid out a swath of interconnected learnings that I believe are important in helping us develop ourselves spiritually, personally and in relationship to ourselves, others and our environment.

So, here we are. We've reached the last chapter of this book. Are you feeling changed as I have promised you would? What has shifted for you? What are you grateful for? I actually want more for you even than to learn you simply read this book. My hope is that you have truly engaged with the different ideas and frameworks introduced here. If you simply enjoyed the read, then I encourage you to go back to a chapter that really spoke to you and work it, integrate it into your being. Try things on that are presented here. But before you accept any ideas and frameworks or reject any ideas and frameworks, test them for yourself. It's important that you take ownership of your experience and your learning. Make it your own.

In the future you may come across stumbling blocks and be tempted to revert to negative behaviors. This is normal and does not mean you are back where you started—even if it sometimes feels that way. Also, sometimes life may suddenly take a turn in a direction you did not want—maybe a long-term relationship has fallen apart or you lost your job. When these kinds of things happen you may question if you have done something wrong. In those instances, we need to remind ourselves that life is ALWAYS for us. From that perspective, we are able to see what seemed like a crisis in the moment was really a blessing—that letting go was necessary to make room for something new, something even better than we had before.

I am also not exempt from these experiences. Sometimes, it can feel like I've forgotten every wise and true thing I've ever learned. When this happens, I simply start all over again with the basics. I get quiet, turn inward and center myself. I remember to ask for help. And when I do, help comes. And I am reminded once again that I live in a loving universe that is here for me.

Our lives are a spiritual journey—an on-going process that requires us to practice, practice, practice—all of the spiritual tools we have learned. And, when I take the time to reflect, I can see that I am in a very different place than I was years before. I can see the progress I've made. There was a time in my life where I was depressed for weeks. Now, it lasts from 30 seconds to maybe 30 minutes!!! That is progress!!! I relish every bit of progress I've made. It encourages me to continue to grow and discover all the new experiences awaiting me. You too are encouraged to take time to celebrate your successes.

Just like me, you arrived here on this planet at this time in history. Thank you for taking this journey with me. Having read this book and started to put its principles into practice, you have done a lot of work. It's time to congratulate yourself. I believe a celebration is in order. In my classes, before I sent our new teachers out into the world to do good, we always had a celebration. I would knight them and together we would sing the song composed by Mitch Leigh with lyrics by Joe Darion, *The Impossible Dream*.

> To dream the impossible dream…
> To run where the brave dare not go…
>
> …To follow that star
> No matter how hopeless,
> No matter how far…

...And the world will be better for this
That we, ...Still strove with our last ounce of courage
To reach the unreachable stars! [1]

So, I knight each of you and send you off to join the forces of love and light at this crucial tipping point. Together we are dreaming the world into its unfolding future. What message, sealed within your heart, do you want to offer to the world? How will you reveal that message tenderly and authentically to both yourself and others? Namaste!

ENDNOTES

Chapter 1

1   Ellen Debenport, *The Five Principles: A Guide to Practical Spirituality*, Unity House,2009.

2   Ellen Debenport, *The Five Principles: A Guide to Practical Spirituality*, Unity House,2009.

3   Neale Donald Walsch, *The Little Soul and the Sun: A Children's Parable*, Hampton Roads Publishing Co.,1998.

4   Taken from an Abraham Hicks recording.

5   Emily Cady, *Lessons in Truth*, Unity Books,1903.

6   James Finley, *Christian Meditation: Experiencing the Presence of God*, HarperCollins Publishers,2005.

Chapter 2

1   Henry David Thoreau quote found at www.goodreads.com.

2   Byron Katie with Stephen Mitchell, *Loving What Is: Four questions that can change your life*, Three Rivers Press, 2002. The actual Judge-Your-Neighbor worksheet can be found on website at www.thework.org.

3   Byron Katie with Stephen Mitchell, *Loving What Is: Four questions that can change your life*, Three Rivers Press, 2002. A printout of the Four questions and the Turn-Around Worksheet can be found on website at www.thework.org.

4   Paul Hasselbeck, *Heart-Centered Metaphysics: A Deeper Look at Unity Teachings*, Unity Books, 2010.

5   Colin Tipping, *Radical Forgiveness: Making Room for the Miracle*, self-published, 2002.

6   Paul Hasselbeck, *Heart-Centered Metaphysics: A Deeper Look at Unity Teachings*, Unity Books, 2010.

7	Joanna Macy and Chris Johnstone, *Active Hope: How to Face the Mess We're in without Going Crazy*, New World Library, 2012.

8	John Seed, quote found in book by Joanna Macy and Chris Johnstone, *Active Hope: How to Face the Mess We're in without Going Crazy*, New World Library, 2012.

9	Dr. Brad Swift, *Life on Purpose: Six Passages to an Inspired Life*, Author's Publishing/Elite Books, 2007.

10	Dr. Brad Swift, *Life on Purpose: Six Passages to an Inspired Life*, Author's Publishing/Elite Books, 2007.

11	Mary Morrisey with Karen Joyce and other great Faculty, *Prosperity Plus…A New Way of Living Participate Guidebook*, Life Solutions That Work, LLC, 2012.

12	Dr. Brad Swift, *Life on Purpose: Six Passages to an Inspired Life*, Author's Publishing/Elite Books, 2007.

Chapter 3

1	Gary Chapman, *The 5 Love Languages: The Secret to Love That Lasts*, Northfield Publishing, 2010.

2	Gary Chapman, *The 5 Love Languages: The Secret to Love That Lasts*, Northfield Publishing, 2010.

3	Kate Large, *The Game of Life Workbook*, DeVorss Publications, 2013.

4	Gary Simmons, *The I of the Storm: Embracing Conflict, Creating Peace*, Unity House, 2001.

5	Jane Simmons, Th.D., *I of the Storm for Teens: Finding Peace in the Midst of Conflict*, The Q Effect Publications, LLC, 2014.

6	Renee Baren & Elizabeth Wagele, *The Enneagram Made Easy*, HarperSanFrancisco, 1994.

7	David Daniels, M.D. & Virginia Price, Ph.D., *The Essential Enneagram*, HarperOne, 2000.

Chapter 4

1	Marshall Rosenberg, Ph.D., *Practical Spirituality*, PuddleDancer Press, 2005.

2	Marshall Rosenberg, Ph.D., *Nonviolent Communication…A Language of Compassion*, PuddleDancer Press, 1999.

3	Linda Dunn, a friend and colleague who is a professor at Elon University where she teaches courses in conflict resolution. She also does Mediation training.

4	Marshall Rosenberg, Ph.D., *Practical Spirituality*, PuddleDancer Press, 2005.

5	Marshall Rosenberg, Ph.D., *Practical Spirituality*, PuddleDancer Press, 2005.

Chapter 5

1   W. H. Murray, *The Scottish Himalayan Expedition*, Chessler Books, 1951.

2   Eric Butterworth, *Spiritual Economics: The Principles and Process of True Prosperity*, Unity House, 2001.

3   Edwene Gaines, *The Four Spiritual Laws of Prosperity: A Simple Guide to Unlimited Abundance*, Rodale, 2005.

4   Mary Morrisey, *Prosperity Plus II—Harnessing Your Invisible Power Participant Guidebook*, LifeSOULutions That Work, LLC, 2013.

5   Ester and Jerry Hicks (The Teachings of Abraham), *Ask and It Is Given: Learning to Manifest Your Desires*, Hay House, Inc, 2004.

6   Ester and Jerry Hicks (The Teachings of Abraham), *Ask and It Is Given: Learning to Manifest Your Desires*, Hay House, Inc, 2004.

7   Meister Eckhart quote found in www.brainquote.com.

Chapter 6

1   Deepak Chopra, *Perfect Health: The Complete Mind/Body Guide*, Harmony Books, 1990.

2   Dr. Eric Pearl, *The Reconnection: Heal Others, Heal Yourself*, Hay House, 2001.

3   Louise Hay, *Heal Your Body: The Mental Causes for Physical Illness and the Metaphysical Way to Overcome Them*, Hay House, Inc., 1982.

4   James Dillet Freeman, *The Story of Unity*, Unity Books, 1978.

5   Thomas E. Witherspoon, *Myrtle Fillmore: Mother of Unity*, Unity Books, 1977.

6   Edwene Gaines, *The Four Spiritual Laws of Prosperity: A Simple Guide to Unlimited Abundance*, Rodale, 2005.

7   Gary Simmons, *The I of the Storm: Embracing Conflict, Creating Peace*, Unity House,2001.

8   Colin Tipping, *Radical Forgiveness: Making Room for the Miracle*, self-published, 2002.

9   Ho'oponopono originated from Hawaii and was originally taught by Mornah Nalamaku Simeona. Mornah was a healer and in 1983 received a great honor by being designated a living treasure.

10 Doc Childre & Howard Martin with Donna Beech, *The HeartMath Solution*, HarperSanFrancisco, 1999.

11 Lynne McTaggart, *The Power of Eight: Harnessing the Miraculous Energies of a Small Group to Heal Others, Your Life, and the World*, Atria Books, 2018.

12 Doc Childre & Howard Martin with Donna Beech, *The HeartMath Solution*, HarperSanFrancisco, 1999.

13 St Teresa of Avila quote in Lynne McTaggart book, *The Power of Eight: Harnessing the Miraculous Energies of a Small Group to Heal Others, Your Life, and the World*, Atria Books, 2018.

14 Dr Charles Tart quote in Lynne McTaggart book, *The Power of Eight: Harnessing the Miraculous Energies of a Small Group to Heal Others, Your Life, and the World,* Atria Books, 2018.

15 Andrew Newberg, M.D. quote in Lynne McTaggart book, *The Power of Eight: Harnessing the Miraculous Energies of a Small Group to Heal Others, Your Life, and the World,* Atria Books, 2018.

16 Lynne McTaggart, *The Power of Eight: Harnessing the Miraculous Energies of a Small Group to Heal Others, Your Life, and the World,* Atria Books, 2018.

Epilogue

1 Adaption of lyrics from Musixmatch, songwriters: Mitch Leigh and Joseph Darion, The Impossible Dream lyrics@ Helena Music Company, Andrew Scott Music, Helena Music Corp.

Made in United States
Orlando, FL
11 February 2023

29865079R00118